BE A BETTER MOTIVATOR

B.K. Pathak

4735/22, Prakash Deep Building
Ansari Road, Darya Ganj,
New Delhi-110002

Lotus Press : Publishers & Distributors
Unit No. 220, 2nd Floor, 4735/22, Prakash Deep Building,
Ansari Road, Darya Ganj, New Delhi- 110002
Ph.: 32903912, 23280047 • E-mail : lotus_press@sify.com
www.lotuspress.co.in

Be a Better Motivator
© 2012, B.K. Pathak
ISBN: 978-81-8382-279-4

Published by : **Lotus Press : Publishers & Distributors** New Delhi-110002
Printed at : Concept Imprint, Delhi

BE A BETTER
MOTIVATOR

Published by:
Lotus Press : Publishers & Distributors

PREFACE

Keeping people motivated is probably one of the biggest challenges that a manager faces. Motivation is an internal feeling which can be understood only by manager since he is in close contact with the employees. Needs, wants and desires are interrelated and they are the driving force to act. These needs can be understood by the manager and he can frame motivation plans accordingly. Motivation therefore is a continuous process since motivation process is based on needs which are unlimited.

One of the main reasons of motivation being a challenging job is due to the changing workforce. The employees become a part of their organization with various needs and expectations. Different employees have different beliefs, attitudes, values, backgrounds and thinking. But all the organizations are not aware of the diversity in their workforce and thus are not aware and clear about different ways of motivating their diverse workforce.

This book, *Be a Better Motivator*, is written for thoughtful leaders, those who wish to work with the grain of human nature rather than against it. It aims to stimulate your own thinking and ideas on this most interesting of all subjects. It should lead you to see some practical ways in which you can better motivate yourself and others.

B. K. Pathak

CONTENTS

Good Environment
Motivated Person

1

IMPORTANCE OF MOTIVATION

Motivation is the word derived from the word 'motive' which means needs, desires, wants or drives within the individuals. It is the process of stimulating people to actions to accomplish the goals. In the work goal context the psychological factors stimulating the people's behaviour can be:

— desire for money
— success
— recognition
— job-satisfaction
— team work, etc.

One of the most important functions of management is to create willingness amongst the employees to perform in the best of their abilities. Therefore the role of a leader is to arouse interest in performance of employees in their jobs. The process of motivation consists of three stages:

— A felt need or drive
— A stimulus in which needs have to be aroused
— When needs are satisfied, the satisfaction or accomplishment of goals.

Therefore, we can say that motivation is a psychological phenomenon which means needs and wants of the individuals have to be tackled by framing an incentive plan.

SIGNIFICANCE OF ORGANIZATIONAL MOTIVATION

Motivation is a very important for an organization because of the following benefits it provides:

Puts Human Resources into Action

Every concern requires physical, financial and human resources to accomplish the goals. It is through motivation that the human resources can be utilized by making full use of it. This can be done by building willingness in employees to work. This will help the enterprise in securing best possible utilization of resources.

Improves Level of Efficiency of Employees

The level of a subordinate or a employee does not only depend upon his qualifications and abilities. For getting best of his work performance, the gap between ability and willingness has to be filled which helps in improving the level of performance of subordinates. This will result into:

— Increase in productivity,

— Reducing cost of operations, and

— Improving overall efficiency.

Leads to Achievement of Organizational Goals

The goals of an enterprise can be achieved only when the following factors take place:

— There is best possible utilization of resources,

— There is a cooperative work environment,

— The employees are goal-directed and they act in a purposive manner.

Goals can be achieved if co-ordination and co-operation takes place simultaneously which can be effectively done through motivation.

Builds Friendly Relationship

Motivation is an important factor which brings employees satisfaction. This can be done by keeping into mind and framing an incentive plan for the benefit of the employees. This could initiate the following things:

— Monetary and non-monetary incentives,

— Promotion opportunities for employees,

— Disincentives for inefficient employees.

In order to build a cordial, friendly atmosphere in a concern, the above steps should be taken by a manager. This would help in:

— Effective cooperation which brings stability,

— Industrial dispute and unrest in employees will reduce,

— The employees will be adaptable to the changes and there will be no resistance to the change,

— This will help in providing a smooth and sound concern in which individual interests will coincide with the organizational interests,

— This will result in profit maximization through increased productivity.

Leads to Stability of Work Force

Stability of workforce is very important from the point of view of reputation and goodwill of a concern. The employees can remain loyal to the enterprise only when they have a feeling of participation in the management. The skills and efficiency of employees will always be of advantage to employees as well as employees. This will lead to a good public image in the market which will attract competent and qualified people into a concern. As it is said, "Old is gold" which suffices with the role of motivation here, the older the people, more the experience and their adjustment into a concern which can be of benefit to the enterprise.

From the above discussion, we can say that motivation is an internal feeling which can be understood only by manager since he is in close contact with the employees. Needs, wants and desires are inter-related and they are the driving force to act. These needs can be understood by the manager and he can frame motivation plans accordingly. We can say that motivation therefore is a continuous process since motivation process is based on needs which are unlimited. The process has to be continued throughout.

We can summarize by saying that motivation is important both to an individual and a business. Motivation is important to an individual as:

— *Motivation will help him achieve his personal goals.*
  — If an individual is motivated, he will have job satisfaction.
  — Motivation will help in self-development of individual.
  — An individual would always gain by working with a dynamic team.
— *Similarly, motivation is important to a business as:*
  — The more motivated the employees are, the more empowered the team is.
  — The more is the team work and individual employee contribution, more profitable and successful is the business.

— During period of amendments, there will be more adaptability and creativity.

— Motivation will lead to an optimistic and challenging attitude at work place.

FEATURES OF A GOOD MOTIVATION SYSTEM

Motivation is a state of mind. High motivation leads to high morale and greater production. A motivated employee gives his best to the organization. He stays loyal and committed to the organization. A sound motivation system in an organization should have the following features:

— Superior performance should be reasonably rewarded and should be duely acknowledged.

— If the performance is not consistently up to the mark, then the system must make provisions for penalties.

— The employees must be dealt in a fair and just manner. The grievances and obstacles faced by them must be dealt instantly and fairly.

— Carrot and stick approach should be implemented to motivate both efficient and inefficient employees. The employees should treat negative consequences (such as fear of punishment) as stick, an outside push and move away from it. They should take positive consequences (such as reward) as carrot, an inner pull and move towards it.

— Performance appraisal system should be very effective.

— Ensure flexibility in working arrangements.

— A sound motivation system must be correlated to organizational goals. Thus, the individual/employee goals must be harmonized with the organizational goals.

— The motivational system must be modified to the situation and to the organization.

— A sound motivation system requires modifying the nature of individual's jobs. The jobs should be redesigned or restructured according to the requirement of situation. Any of the alternatives to job specialization—job rotation, job enlargement, job enrichment, etc. could be used.

— The management approach should be participative. All the subordinates and employees should be involved in decision-making process.

— The motivation system should involve monetary as well as non-monetary rewards. The monetary rewards should be correlated to performance. Performance should be based on the employees' action towards the goals, and not on the fame of employees.

— "Motivate yourself to motivate your employees" should be the managerial approach.

— The managers must understand and identify the motivators for each employee.

— Sound motivation system should encourage supportive supervision whereby the supervisors share their views and experiences with their subordinates, listen to the subordinates views, and assist the subordinates in performing the designated job.

MOTIVATION AND MORALE

Morale can be defined as the total satisfaction derived by an individual from his job, his work-group, his superior, the organization he works for and the environment. It generally relates to the feeling of individual's comfort, happiness and satisfaction. According to Davis, "Morale is a mental condition of groups and individuals which determines their attitude."In short, morale is a fusion of employees' attitudes, behaviours, manifestation of views and opinions—all taken together in their work scenarios, exhibiting the employees' feelings towards work, working terms and relation with their employers. Morale includes employees' attitudes on and specific reaction to their job.

There are two states of morale:

High Morale

High morale implies determination at work- an essential in achievement of management objectives. High morale results in:

— A keen teamwork on part of the employees.
— Organizational Commitment and a sense of belongingness in the employees mind.
— Immediate conflict identification and resolution.
— Healthy and safe work environment.
— Effective communication in the organization.
— Increase in productivity.
— Greater motivation.

Low Morale

Low morale has following features:

— Greater grievances and conflicts in organization.
— High rate of employee absenteeism and turnover.
— Dissatisfaction with the superiors and employers.
— Poor working conditions.
— Employees frustration.
— Decrease in productivity.
— Lack of motivation.

Though motivation and morale are closely related concepts, they are different in following ways:

— While motivation is an internal-psychological drive of an individual which urges him to behave in a specific manner, morale is more of a group scenario.

— Higher motivation often leads to higher morale of employees, but high morale does not essentially result in greatly motivated employees as to have a positive attitude towards all factors of work situation may not essentially force the employees to work more efficiently.

— While motivation is an individual concept, morale is a group concept. Thus, motivation takes into consideration the individual differences among the employees, and morale of the employees can be increased by taking those factors into consideration which influence group scenario or total work settings.

— Motivation acquires primary concern in every organization, while morale is a secondary phenomenon because high motivation essentially leads to higher productivity while high morale may not necessarily lead to higher productivity.

— Things tied to morale are usually things that are just part of the work environment, and things tied to motivation are tied to the performance of the individual.

FIFTY-FIFTY RULE IN MOTIVATION

The Fifty-Fifty Rule in motivation cas be stated as follows:

Fifty per cent of motivation comes from within a person and 50 per cent from his or her environment, especially from the leadership encountered there.

The Fifty-Fifty Rule in motivation does not claim to identify the different proportions in the equation exactly. It is more like a rough-and-ready rule of thumb. In effect is says no more than that a substantial part of motivation lies within a person while a substantial part lies, so to speak, outside and beyond control. A child, for example, might have a potential interest in science and be generally ambitious to do well at school and go to university. But the Fifty-Fifty Rule comes into play. Fifty per cent of the child's progress will depend upon the academic quality of the school and in particular upon the personality and ability of the science teacher. A great schoolteacher has been defined as 'one whose actual lessons may be forgotten, but whose living enthusiasm is a quickening, animating and inspiring power'.

The Fifty-Fifty Rule does have the benefit of reminding leaders that they have a key part to play—for good or ill—in the motivation of people at work. Fortunately not all the cards are in their hands, for they are dealing with people who are self-motivating in various degrees. The art of readership is to work with the natural grain of the particular wood of humanity which comes to hand. Selection is important, for—in the blunt words of the Spanish proverb—'You cannot carve rotten wood.' Apart from individual needs there are other needs emanating from the common task and the group or organization involved which have at least a potential motivational influence upon us. The value, worthwhileness or importance of the work are doing, in the context of a changing and challenging environment, can enlist deepest interest and engage purposive energy.

The Fifty-Fifty Rule is an invitation to get your part in the motivational relationship right. Doubtless, like the Pareto Principle, other applications of the Fifty-Fifty Rule will soon be discovered. It applies to the relative values of leadership and teamwork: 50 per cent of success depends on the team and 50 per cent on the leader. Again these are not scientific proportions. But they do indicate just how substantial is each contribution, regardless of that made by the other party. Here the Fifty-Fifty Rule challenges the leader to get his or her part right first before criticizing the quality of contribution of the other party. It is the ultimate cure to the 'Us and Them' disease of organizations. About half destiny depends upon inherited characteristics or tendencies; the other half depends upon what make of them. In the second part of that proposition lies the real challenge to parents and teachers. Certainly that applies in the leadership field. The idea that leaders are born and not made is a half truth. The full truth is that they are (about) half born and (more-or-less) half made -by experience and thought, by training and practice. This mixture of self-teaching and teaching by others of course takes a lifetime. For paradoxically it takes a long time to become a natural leader.

The Fifty-Fifty Rule ties in well with the meaning of the word 'motivation'. In fact, it is a relatively new word, being introduced in the 1940s. Like the native English word 'motive' it can be used as a neutral explanation of cause: what motivated him to commit the murder? Or it can indicate a conscious desire or inculcate a desire for something or other: students motivated to learn by the encouragement of a good teacher. Motivation is closer in meaning to the older English concept of motivity: the power of initiating or producing movement. All these words—motive, motivation, motivity—come from the Latin verb 'to move'. What moves us to action may come from within or from without, or—more commonly—from some combination of inner impulse or proclivity on the one hand and outer situations or stimuli on the other. The merit, then, of 'motivation' as a word is that it fits perfectly the Fifty-Fifty Rule. For it covers both what happens inside individuals in terms of wanting to do something and also what happens outside them as they are influenced by others or by circumstances. When someone is motivating you, he or she is consciously or unconsciously seeking to change the strength and/or direction of your motive energy. This second aspect of motivation does raise an ethical issue. But this human dependency on others can be used for own ends. How does legitimate influence differ from manipulation?

To manipulate someone means to control or play upon him or her by artful, unfair or insidious means, especially to one's own advantage. Therefore there are two aspects of manipulation: the means and the ends. If it is *your* purpose and not a common purpose that is being served, you are running into the danger of manipulation. If the means you employ to motivate others are hidden from them or seek to bypass their conscious minds, then one is becoming a manipulator rather than a motivator. Motivating others, therefore, should not be confused with manipulatory practices used by strong personalities to dominate weaker ones. Leadership exists in its most natural form among equals. It is not the same as domination or the exercise of power. True leaders respect the integrity of others. Bosses demand respect; leaders give respect. Granted such a relationship, based upon mutual trust and supported by a common sense of justice or fairness, then it is part of the responsibility of leaders to stir up enthusiasm for the common task.

2

THEORIES OF MOTIVATION

CLASSICAL THEORIES OF MOTIVATION

The motivation concepts were mainly developed around 1950's. Three main theories were made during this period. These three classical theories are:

— Maslow's Hierarchy of Needs Theory

— Herzberg's Two Factor Theory

— Douglas MacGragor's Theory X and Theory Y

These theories are building blocks of the contemporary theories developed later. The working mangers and learned professionals till date use these classical theories to explain the concept of employee motivation.

Maslow's Hierarchy of Needs

Abraham Maslow is well renowned for proposing the Hierarchy of Needs Theory in 1943. This theory is a classical depiction of human motivation. This theory is based on the assumption that there is a hierarchy of five needs within each individual. The urgency of these needs varies. These five needs are as follows:

1. *Physiological needs*: These are the basic needs of air, water, food, clothing and shelter. In other words,

physiological needs are the needs for basic amenities of life.

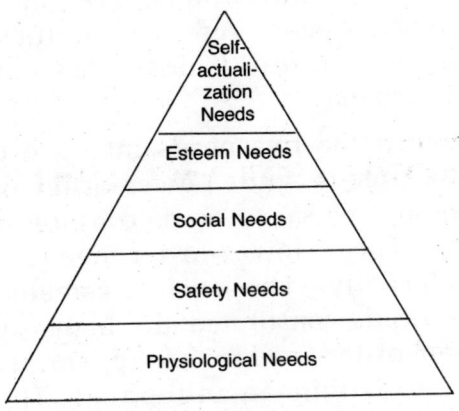

Maslow's Need Hierarchy Model

2. *Safety needs*: Safety needs include physical, environmental and emotional safety and protection. For instance—Job security, financial security, protection from animals, family security, health security, etc.

3. *Social needs*: Social needs include the need for love, affection, care, belongingness, and friendship.

4. *Esteem needs*: Esteem needs are of two types: internal esteem needs (self-respect, confidence, competence, achievement and freedom) and external esteem needs (recognition, power, status, attention and admiration).

5. *Self-actualization need*: This include the urge to become what you are capable of becoming / what you have the potential to become. It includes the need for growth and self-contentment. It also includes desire for gaining more knowledge, social-service, creativity and being aesthetic. The self-actualization needs are never fully satiable. As an

individual grows psychologically, opportunities keep cropping up to continue growing. According to Maslow, individuals are motivated by unsatisfied needs. As each of these needs is significantly satisfied, it drives and forces the next need to emerge.

Maslow grouped the five needs into two categories— Higher-order needs and Lower-order needs. The physiological and the safety needs constituted the lower-order needs. These lower-order needs are mainly satisfied externally. The social, esteem, and self-actualization needs constituted the higher-order needs. These higher-order needs are generally satisfied internally, i.e., within an individual. Thus, we can conclude that during boom period, the employees lower-order needs are significantly met.

Physiological Needs

The concept of physiological drives has usually been taken as the starting point for motivational theory. Maslow advocated the use of the word 'need' as an alternative to 'drive', basing his case on the notion of physical homeostasis, the body's natural effort to maintain a constant normal state of the bloodstream, coupled with the finding that appetites in the sense of preferential choices of good are a fairly efficient indicator of actual deficiencies in the body. Not all physiological needs were homeostatic, for the list could be extended to include sexual desire, sleepiness, sheer activity and maternal behaviour in animals. Indeed, if a growing loss of specificity in description were acceptable, he held that it would be possible to extend the list of physiological needs very considerably.

For two reasons Maslow considered the physical needs to be unique rather than typical of the basic human needs. First, they could be regarded as relatively independent of one another and other orders of need. Second, in the classic cases of hunger, thirst and sex, there was a localized physical base for the need. Yet this relative uniqueness could be equated with isolation: the physiological needs might serve as channels for all sorts of other needs as well. The man who thinks he is hungry, for example, may be looking for security rather than carbohydrates or proteins. If a man becomes chronically short of food and water he becomes dominated by the desire to eat and to drink, and his concern for other needs tends to be swept away. Thus the physiological needs are the most prepotent of all needs. What this prepotence means precisely is that the human being who is missing everything in life in an extreme fashion will still tend to seek satisfaction for his or her physiological needs rather than any others. Under such temporary dominance a person's whole attitude to the future may undergo change: 'For our chronically and extremely hungry man, Utopia can be defined simply as a place where there is plenty of food ... Such a man may fairly be said to live by bread alone.'

Supposing, however, a person has plenty of food guaranteed to him or her in the foreseeable future. Then, declared Maslow, another unsatisfied need emerges to dominate the organism. In other words, a satisfied want ceases to motivate. If a person has an endless supply of bread, at once other needs emerge and they supersede the physiological needs in dominating the organism. And when these in turn are satisfied, yet higher needs emerge, and so on. This is what Maslow meant by asserting that the basic human needs are organized into a hierarchy of relative prepotency. Maslow entered an early caveat against a possible misinterpretation of his theory by advancing the hypothesis that individuals in whom a certain need had always been gratified would be the best equipped to tolerate a later frustration in that area. On the other hand, those who had been deprived would respond in a different way to eventual satisfaction than those who had been more fortunate in their younger days.

Safety Needs

When the physiological needs are relatively well satisfied, a new set of needs emerges centred upon the safety of the organism. Owing to the inhibition by adults of any signs of reaction to threat or danger this aspect of human behaviour is more easily observed in children, who react in a total manner to any sudden disturbance, such as being dropped, startled by loud noises, flashing lights, by rough handling, or by inadequate support. Maslow found other indications for the need of safety in a child's preference for routine or rhythm, for a predictable and orderly world. Injustice, unfairness or lack of consistency in the parents seem to make a child feel anxious and unsafe. 'This attitude may be not so much because of the injustice *per se* or any particular pains involved; but rather because this treatment threatens to make the world look unreliable, or unsafe, or unpredictable.' The consensus of informed opinion held that children thrived best upon a limited permissiveness, for they need an organized or structured world. The sight of strange, unfamiliar or uncontrollable objects, illness or death can elicit fear responses in children. 'Particularly at such times, the child's frantic clinging to his parents is eloquent testimony to their role as protectors.'

Another attempt to seek safety and stability in the world may be seen in the very common preference for familiar rather than unfamiliar things, or for the known rather than the unknown. Maslow added also the common suggestion that the appeal of religions and philosophies, which organize the universe and the people in it into some sort of coherent whole, may in part stem from this universal human need for safety and security. Neurotic individuals may be characterized as adults who have retained their childish attitudes to the world. They perceive the world as hostile, overwhelming and threatening. Their urge towards safety or escape may take the form of a search for some strong all-powerful protector, or become a frantic effort to order the world so that no unexpected or unfamiliar dangers will ever appear. All sorts of ceremonials, rules and formulas might be employed so that every possible contingency is guarded against. Doubtless, however, Maslow would have allowed that rituals and rules could perform quite different functions for healthy or mature people.

Social Needs

If the physiological and safety needs are met, then the needs for love, affection and belongingness emerge as the dominant centre of motivation. The person concerned will feel keenly the absence of friends, wife or children; he will strive for affectionate relations with people and for 'a place in his group'. Although Maslow distinguished between love and sex, and he showed an awareness that love needs to involve both giving and receiving love, it is an important characteristic of his psychology that he generally reserved the use of the word 'love' for close personal relationships. There is much to be said for following later practice and calling this set the 'Social Needs'.

Esteem Needs

This order includes both the need or desire for a high evaluation of self and for the esteem of others. Maslow divided them into two subsidiary sets:

- The desire for strength, achievement, adequacy, mastery, competence, confidence in the face of the world, independence, and freedom; and

— The desire for reputation, prestige, status, dominance, recognition, attention, importance and appreciation.

From theological discussions of *hubris* as well as from such sources as the writings of Eric Fromm, Maslow believed that:

> We have been learning more and more of the dangers of basing self-esteem on the opinions of others rather than on real capacity, competence, and adequacy to the task. The most stable and therefore most healthy self-esteem is based on *deserved* respect from others rather than on external fame or celebrity and unwarranted adulation.

Need for Self-Actualization

Even if all these needs are satisfied, we may still often expect that a new discontent and restlessness will soon develop, unless the individual is doing what he is fitted for. A musician must make music, an artist must paint, a poet must write, if he is to be ultimately at peace with himself. What a man can be, he must be. This need we may call self-actualization. It refers to man's desire for self-fulfilment, namely, to the tendency for him to become actualized in what he is potentially. This tendency might be phrased as the desire to become more and more what one is, to become everything that one is capable of becoming...

The clear emergence of these needs usually rests upon prior satisfaction of the physiological, safety, love and esteem needs.

Desires to Know and Understand

Maslow allowed that there were two other sets of needs which found no place in the above hierarchical order, and he felt it necessary to recognize them while make it clear that at present psychologists had little to say about them. He suggested, however, that the principle of a hierarchy of prepotency might also apply in both cases, albeit in a shadowy form. In contemporary presentations of Maslow's theory of needs in management education, these two scales are usually and unfortunately omitted altogether. It should be noted also that there is some ambiguity about Maslow's language at this point. When he wrote about 'higher needs' he is sometimes referring to esteem and self-actualization; at other times, however, he has in mind the cognitive and aesthetic needs described below.

Maslow began marshalling the evidence for such desires by noting the presence of 'something like human curiosity' in monkeys and apes. He continued:

> Studies of psychologically healthy people indicate that they are, as a defining characteristic, attracted to the mysterious, to the unknown, to the chaotic, unorganized, and unexplained. This seems to be a *per se* attractiveness; these areas are in themselves and of their own right interesting. The contrasting reaction to the well-known is one of boredom.

The gratification of the cognitive impulses is subjectively satisfying. Moreover,

> Even after we know, we are impelled to know more and more minutely and microscopically on the one hand, and on the other, more and more extensively in the direction of a world philosophy, theology etc. The facts that we acquire, if they are isolated or atomistic, inevitably get theorized about, and either analysed or organized or both. This process has been phrased by some as the search for meaning. We shall then postulate a desire to understand, to systematize, to organize, to analyse, to look for relations and meanings, to construct a system of values.

Maslow concluded with a warning against making a too sharp dichotomy between the cognitive and the conative (or basic needs) hierarchies.

Aesthetic Needs

Maslow was convinced that:

> In *some* individuals there is a truly basic aesthetic need. They get sick (in special ways) from ugliness, and are cured by beautiful surroundings; they *crave* actively, and their cravings can be satisfied *only* by beauty. It is seen almost universally in healthy children. Some evidence of such as impulse is found in every culture and in every age as far back as the cavemen.

The conative, cognitive and aesthetic needs overlap so much that it is impossible to separate them sharply.

> The needs for order, for symmetry, for closure, for completion of the art, for system, and for structure may be indiscriminately assigned *either* to cognitive, conative, or aesthetic, or even to neurotic needs.

Coping and Expressive Behaviour

Lastly, Maslow expounded a useful distinction between coping and expressive behaviour which does not try to do anything: 'it is simply a reflection of the personality'. As examples of expressive or non-functional behaviour, Maslow listed 'the random movements of a healthy child, the smile on the face of a happy man even when he is alone, the springiness of the healthy man's walk, and the erectness of his carriage'. Moreover, the style in which a person behaves may or may not be expressive. Yet even here Maslow warned against a false dichotomy: 'It is finally necessary to stress that expressiveness of behaviour and goal-directedness of behaviour are not mutually exclusive categories.

Implications of Maslow's Theory for Managers

— As far as the physiological needs are concerned, the managers should give employees appropriate salaries to purchase the basic necessities of life. Breaks and eating opportunities should be given to employees.

— As far as the safety needs are concerned, the managers should provide the employees job security, safe and hygienic work environment, and retirement benefits so as to retain them.

— As far as social needs are concerned, the management should encourage teamwork and organize social events.

— As far as esteem needs are concerned, the managers can appreciate and reward employees on accomplishing and exceeding their targets. The management can give the deserved employee higher job rank / position in the organization.

— As far as self-actualization needs are concerned, the managers can give the employees challenging jobs in which the employees' skills and competencies are fully utilized. Moreover, growth opportunities can be given to them so that they can reach the peak.

The managers must identify the need level at which the employee is existing and then those needs can be utilized as push for motivation.

Limitations of Maslow's Theory

— It is essential to note that not all employees are governed by same set of needs. Different individuals may be driven by different needs at same point of time. It is always the most powerful unsatisfied need that motivates an individual.

- The theory is not empirically supported.
- The theory is not applicable in case of starving artist as even if the artist's basic needs are not satisfied, he will still strive for recognition and achievement.

Herzberg's Two-Factor Theory of Motivation

In 1959, Frederick Herzberg, a behavioural scientist proposed a two-factor theory or the motivator-hygiene theory. According to Herzberg, there are some job factors that result in satisfaction while there are other job factors that prevent dissatisfaction. According to Herzberg, the opposite of "Satisfaction" is "No satisfaction" and the opposite of "Dissatisfaction" is "No Dissatisfaction".

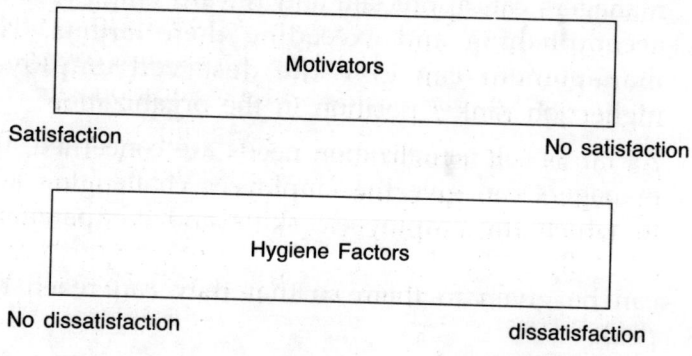

Herzberg's view of satisfaction and dissatisfaction

Herzberg classified these job factors into two categories:

Hygiene Factors

Hygiene factors are those job factors which are essential for existence of motivation at workplace. These do not lead to positive satisfaction for long-term. But if these factors are absent/ if these factors are non-existant at workplace, then they lead to dissatisfaction. In other words, hygiene factors are those factors which when adequate/ reasonable in a job, pacify the employees and do not make them dissatisfied. These factors are extrinsic to work. Hygiene factors are also called as dissatisfiers or maintenance factors as they are required to avoid dissatisfaction. These factors describe the job environment/ scenario. The hygiene factors symbolized the physiological needs which the individuals wanted and expected to be fulfilled. Hygiene factors include:

— *Pay*: The pay or salary structure should be appropriate and reasonable. It must be equal and competitive to those in the same industry in the same domain.

— *Company policies and administrative policies*: The company policies should not be too rigid. They should be fair and clear. It should include flexible working hours, dress code, breaks, vacation, etc.

— *Fringe benefits*: The employees should be offered health care plans (mediclaim), benefits for the family members, employee help programmes, etc.

— *Physical working condition*: The working conditions should be safe, clean and hygienic. The work equipments should be updated and well-maintained.

— *Status*: The employees' status within the organization should be familiar and retained.

— *Interpersonal relations*: The relationship of the employees with his peers, superiors and subordinates should be appropriate and acceptable. There should be no conflict or humiliation element present.

— *Job security*: The organization must provide job security to the employees.

Implications of Two-Factor Theory

The Two-Factor theory implies that the managers must stress upon guaranteeing the adequacy of the hygiene factors to avoid employee dissatisfaction. Also, the managers must make sure that the work is stimulating and rewarding so that the employees are motivated to work and perform harder and better. This theory emphasize upon job-enrichment so as to motivate the employees. The job must utilize the employee's skills and competencies to the maximum. Focusing on the motivational factors can improve work-quality.

Limitations of Two-Factor Theory

The two factor theory is not free from limitations:

- The two-factor theory overlooks situational variables.
- Herzberg assumed a correlation between satisfaction and productivity. But the research conducted by Herzberg stressed upon satisfaction and ignored productivity.
- The theory's reliability is uncertain. Analysis has to be made by the raters. The raters may spoil the findings by analyzing same response in different manner.
- No comprehensive measure of satisfaction was used. An employee may find his job acceptable despite the fact that he may hate/object part of his job.
- The two-factor theory is not free from bias as it is based on the natural reaction of employees when they are enquired the sources of satisfaction and dissatisfaction at work. They will blame dissatisfaction on the external factors such as salary structure, company policies and peer relationship.

Also, the employees will give credit to themselves for the satisfaction factor at work.

— The theory ignores blue-collar workers. Despite these limitations, Herzberg's Two-Factor Theory is acceptable broadly.

Douglas McGregor's Theory X and Theory Y

In 1960, Douglas McGregor formulated Theory X and Theory Y suggesting two aspects of human behaviour at work, or in other words, two different views of individuals (employees): one of which is negative, called as Theory X and the other is positive, so called as Theory Y. According to McGregor, the perception of managers on the nature of individuals is based on various assumptions.

Assumptions of Theory X

— An average employee intrinsically does not like work and tries to escape it whenever possible.

— Since the employee does not want to work, he must be persuaded, compelled, or warned with punishment so as to achieve organizational goals. A close supervision is required on part of managers. The managers adopt a more dictatorial style.

— Many employees rank job security on top, and they have little or no aspiration/ambition.

— Employees generally dislike responsibilities.

— Employees resist change.

— An average employee needs formal direction.

Assumptions of Theory Y

— Employees can perceive their job as relaxing and normal. They exercise their physical and mental efforts in an inherent manner in their jobs.

- Employees may not require only threat, external control and coercion to work, but they can use self-direction and self-control if they are dedicated and sincere to achieve the organizational objectives.

- If the job is rewarding and satisfying, then it will result in employees' loyalty and commitment to organization.

- An average employee can learn to admit and recognize the responsibility. In fact, he can even learn to obtain responsibility.

- The employees have skills and capabilities. Their logical capabilities should be fully utilized. In other words, the creativity, resourcefulness and innovative potentiality of the employees can be utilized to solve organizational problems.

Thus, we can say that Theory X presents a pessimistic view of employees' nature and behaviour at work, while Theory Y presents an optimistic view of the employees' nature and behaviour at work. If correlate it with Maslow's theory, we can say that Theory X is based on the assumption that the employees emphasize on the physiological needs and the safety needs; while Theory X is based on the assumption that the social needs, esteem needs and the self-actualization needs dominate the employees.

McGregor views Theory Y to be more valid and reasonable than Theory X. Thus, he encouraged cordial team relations, responsible and stimulating jobs, and participation of all in decision-making process.

Implications of Theory X and Theory Y

- Quite a few organizations use Theory X today. Theory X encourages use of tight control and supervision. It implies that employees are reluctant to organizational changes. Thus, it does not encourage innovation.

— Many organizations are using Theory Y techniques. Theory Y implies that the managers should create and encourage a work environment which provides opportunities to employees to take initiative and self-direction. Employees should be given opportunities to contribute to organizational well-being. Theory Y encourages decentralization of authority, teamwork and participative decision making in an organization. Theory Y searches and discovers the ways in which an employee can make significant contributions in an organization. It harmonizes and matches employees' needs and aspirations with organizational needs and aspirations.

MODERN THEORIES OF MOTIVATION

We all are familiar with the classical theories of motivation, but they all are not empirically supported. As far as contemporary theories of motivation are concerned, all are well supported with evidences. Some of the contemporary/modern theories of motivation are explained below.

ERG Theory of Motivation

To bring Maslow's need hierarchy theory of motivation in synchronization with empirical research, Clayton Alderfer redefined it in his own terms. His rework is called as ERG theory of motivation. He recategorized Maslow's hierarchy of needs into three simpler and broader classes of needs:

— *Existence needs:* These include need for basic material necessities. In short, it includes an individual's physiological and physical safety needs.

— *Relatedness needs:* These include the aspiration individual's have for maintaining significant interpersonal relationships (be it with family, peers or superiors), getting public fame and recognition. Maslow's social needs and external component of esteem needs fall under this class of need.

— *Growth needs:* These include need for self-development and personal growth and advancement. Maslow's self-actualization needs and intrinsic component of esteem needs fall under this category of need.

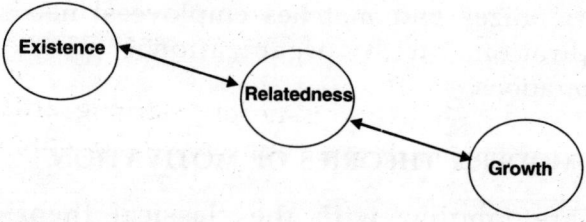

The significance of the three classes of needs may vary for each individual.

Difference between Maslow's Theory and ERG Theory

— ERG Theory states that at a given point of time, more than one need may be operational.

— ERG Theory also shows that if the fulfilment of a higher-level need is subdued, there is an increase in desire for satisfying a lower-level need.

— According to Maslow, an individual remains at a particular need level until that need is satisfied. While according to ERG theory, if a higher level need aggravates, an individual may revert to increase the satisfaction of a lower-level need. This is called frustration- regression aspect of ERG theory. For instance—when growth need aggravates, then an individual might be motivated to accomplish the relatedness need and if there are issues in accomplishing relatedness needs, then he might be motivated by the existence needs. Thus, frustration/aggravation can result in regression to a lower-level need.

— While Maslow's need hierarchy theory is rigid as it assumes that the needs follow a specific and orderly hierarchy and unless a lower-level need is satisfied, an individual cannot proceed to the higher-level need; ERG Theory of motivation is very flexible as he perceived the needs as a range/variety rather than perceiving them as a hierarchy. According to Alderfer, an individual can work on growth needs even if his existence or relatedness needs remain unsatisfied. Thus, he gives explanation to the issue of "starving artist" who can struggle for growth even if he is hungry.

Implications of the ERG Theory

Managers must understand that an employee has various needs that must be satisfied at the same time. According to the ERG theory, if the manager concentrates solely on one need at a time, this will not effectively motivate the employee. Also, the frustration- regression aspect of ERG Theory has an added effect on workplace motivation. For instance—if an employee is not provided with growth and advancement opportunities in an organization, he might revert to the relatedness need such as socializing needs and to meet those socializing needs, if the environment or circumstances do not permit, he might revert to the need for money to fulfil those socializing needs. The sooner the manager realizes and discovers this, the more immediate steps they will take to fulfill those needs which are frustrated until such time that the employee can again pursue growth.

McClelland's Theory of Needs

David McClelland and his associates proposed McClelland's theory of Needs/Achievement Motivation Theory. This theory states that human behaviour is affected by three needs—Need for Power, Achievement and Affiliation. Need for achievement is the urge to excel, to accomplish in relation to a set of standards, to struggle to achieve success. Need for power is the desire to influence other individual's behaviour as per your wish. In other words, it is the desire to have control over others and to be influential. Need for affiliation is a need for open and sociable interpersonal relationships. In other words, it is a desire for relationship based on co-operation and mutual understanding.The individuals with high achievement needs are highly motivated by competing and challenging work. They look for promotional opportunities in job. They have a strong urge for feedback on their achievement. Such individuals try to get satisfaction in performing things better. High achievement is directly related to high performance. Individuals who are better and above average performers are highly motivated. They assume responsibility for solving the problems at work. McClelland called such individuals as gamblers as they set challenging targets for themselves and they take deliberate risk to achieve those set targets. Such individuals look for innovative ways of performing job. They perceive achievement of goals as a reward, and value it more than a financial reward.

The individuals who are motivated by power have a strong urge to be influential and controlling. They want that their views and ideas should dominate and thus, they want to lead. Such individuals are motivated by the need for reputation and self-esteem. Individuals with greater power and authority will perform better than those possessing less power. Generally, managers with high need for power turn out to be more efficient and successful managers. They are more determined and loyal to the organization they work for. Need for power should not always be taken negatively. It can be viewed as the need to have a positive effect on the organization and to support the organization in achieving it's goals.

The individuals who are motivated by affiliation have an urge for a friendly and supportive environment. Such individuals are effective performers in a team. These people want to be liked by others. The manager's ability to make decisions is hampered if they have a high affiliation need as they prefer to be accepted and liked by others, and this weakens their objectivity. Individuals having high affiliation needs prefer working in an environment providing greater personal interaction. Such people have a need to be on the good books of all. They generally cannot be good leaders.

Goal Setting Theory of Motivation

In 1960's, *Edwin Locke* put forward the Goal-setting Theory of Motivation. This theory states that goal setting is essentially linked to task performance. It states that specific and challenging goals along with appropriate feedback contribute to higher and better task performance. In simple words, goals indicate and give direction to an employee about what needs to be done and how much efforts are required to be put in. The important features of goal-setting theory are as follows:

- The willingness to work towards attainment of goal is main source of job motivation. Clear, particular and difficult goals are greater motivating factors than easy, general and vague goals.

- Specific and clear goals lead to greater output and better performance. Unambiguous, measurable and clear goals accompanied by a deadline for completion avoids misunderstanding.

— Goals should be realistic and challenging. This gives an individual a feeling of pride and triumph when he attains them, and sets him up for attainment of next goal. The more challenging the goal, the greater is the reward generally and the more is the passion for achieving it.

— Better and appropriate feedback of results directs the employee behaviour and contributes to higher performance than absence of feedback. Feedback is a means of gaining reputation, making clarifications and regulating goal difficulties. It helps employees to work with more involvement and leads to greater job satisfaction.

— Employees' participation in goal is not always desirable.

— Participation of setting goal, however, makes goal more acceptable and leads to more involvement.

— Goal setting theory has certain eventualities such as:

    — *Self-efficiency*—Self-efficiency is the individual's self-confidence and faith that he has potential of performing the task. Higher the level of self-efficiency, greater will be the efforts put in by the individual when they face challenging tasks. While, lower the level of self-efficiency, less will be the efforts put in by the individual or he might even quit while meeting challenges.

    — *Goal commitment*—Goal setting theory assumes that the individual is committed to the goal and will not leave the goal. The goal commitment is dependent on the following factors: Goals are made open, known and broadcasted. Goals should be set-self by individual rather than designated. Individual's set goals should be consistent with the organizational goals and vision.

Advantages of Goal Setting Theory

— Goal setting theory is a technique used to raise incentives for employees to complete work quickly and effectively.

— Goal setting leads to better performance by increasing motivation and efforts, but also through increasing and improving the feedback quality.

Limitations of Goal Setting Theory

— At times, the organizational goals are in conflict with the managerial goals. Goal conflict has a detrimental effect on the performance if it motivates incompatible action drift.

— Very difficult and complex goals stimulate riskier behaviour.

— If the employee lacks skills and competencies to perform actions essential for goal, then the goal-setting can fail and lead to undermining of performance.

— There is no evidence to prove that goal-setting improves job satisfaction.

Reinforcement Theory of Motivation

Reinforcement theory of motivation was proposed by BF Skinner and his associates. It states that individual's behaviour is a function of its consequences. It is based on "law of effect", i.e, individual's behaviour with positive consequences tends to be repeated, but individual's behaviour with negative consequences tends not to be repeated. Reinforcement theory of motivation overlooks the internal state of individual, i.e., the inner feelings and drives of individuals are ignored by Skinner. This theory focuses totally on what happens to an individual when he takes some action. Thus, according to Skinner, the external environment of the organization must be designed effectively and positively so as to motivate the employee. This theory is a strong tool for analyzing controlling mechanism for individual's behaviour. However, it does not focus on the causes of individual's behaviour.

The managers use the following methods for controlling the behaviour of the employees:

— *Positive Reinforcement:* This implies giving a positive response when an individual shows positive and required behaviour. For example—Immediately praising an employee for coming early for job. This will increase probability of outstanding behaviour occurring again. Reward is a positive reinforce, but not necessarily. If and only if the employees' behaviour improves, reward can said to be a positive reinforcer. Positive reinforcement stimulates occurrence of a behaviour. It must be noted that more spontaneous is the giving of reward, the greater reinforcement value it has.

— *Negative Reinforcement:* This implies rewarding an employee by removing negative/undesirable consequences. Both positive and negative reinforcement can be used for increasing desirable / required behaviour.

— *Punishment:* It implies removing positive consequences so as to lower the probability of repeating undesirable behaviour in future. In other words, punishment means applying undesirable consequence for showing undesirable behaviour. For instance—Suspending an employee for breaking the organizational rules. Punishment can be equalized by positive reinforcement from alternative source.

— *Extinction:* It implies absence of reinforcements. In other words, extinction implies lowering the probability of undesired behaviour by removing reward for that kind of behaviour. For instance—if an employee no longer receives praise and admiration for his good work, he may feel that his behaviour is generating no fruitful consequence.

Implications of Reinforcement Theory

Reinforcement theory explains in detail how an individual learns behaviour. Managers who are making attempt to motivate the employees must ensure that they do not reward all employees simultaneously. They must tell the employees what they are not doing correct. They must tell the employees how they can achieve positive reinforcement.

Equity Theory of Motivation

The core of the equity theory is the principle of balance or equity. As per this motivation theory, an individual's motivation level is correlated to his perception of equity, fairness and justice practiced by the management. Higher is individual's perception of fairness, greater is the motivation level and vice versa. While evaluating fairness, employee compares the job input (in terms of contribution) to outcome (in terms of compensation) and also compares the same with that of another peer of equal cadre/category. O/I ratio (output-input ratio) is used to make such a comparison.

Equity Theory	
Ratio Comparison	*Perception*
O/I a < O/I b	Under-rewarded (Equity Tension)
O/I a = O/I b	Equity
O/I a > O/I b	Over-rewarded (Equity Tension)

Negative Tension state: Equity is perceived when this ratio is equal. While if this ratio is unequal, it leads to "equity tension". J. Stacy Adams called this a negative tension state which motivates him to do something right to relieve this tension. A comparison has been made between two workers A and B to understand this point.

Referents: The four comparisons an employee can make have been termed as "referents" according to Goodman. The referent chosen is a significant variable in equity theory. These referents are as follows:

— *Self-inside*: An employee's experience in a different position inside his present organization.

— *Self-outside*: An employee's experience in a situation outside the present organization.

— *Other-inside*: Another employee or group of employees inside the employee's present organization.

— *Other-outside*: Another employee or employees outside the employee's present organization.

An employee might compare himself with his peer within the present job in the current organization or with his friend/peer working in some other organization or with the past jobs held by him with others. An employee's choice of the referent will be influenced by the appeal of the referent and the employee's knowledge about the referent.

Moderating Variables: The gender, salary, education and the experience level are moderating variables. Individuals with greater and higher education are more informed. Thus, they are likely to compare themselves with the outsiders. Males and females prefer same sex comparison. It has been observed that females are paid typically less than males in comparable jobs and have less salary expectations than male for the same work. Thus, a women employee that uses another women employee as a referent tends to lead to a lower comparative standard.

Employees with greater experience know their organization very well and compare themselves with their own colleagues, while employees with less experience rely on their personal experiences and knowledge for making comparisons.

Choices: The employees who perceive inequity and are under negative tension can make the following choices:

— Change in input (e.g. Don't overexert)

— Change their outcome (Produce quantity output and increasing earning by sacrificing quality when piece rate incentive system exist)

— Choose a different referent

— Quit the job

— Change self perception (For instance—I know that I've performed better and harder than everyone else.)

— Change perception of others (For instance—Jack's job is not as desirable as I earlier thought it was.)

Assumptions of the Equity Theory

— The theory demonstrates that the individuals are concerned both with their own rewards and also with what others get in their comparison.

— Employees expect a fair and equitable return for their contribution to their jobs.

— Employees decide what their equitable return should be after comparing their inputs and outcomes with those of their colleagues.

— Employees who perceive themselves as being in an inequitable scenario will attempt to reduce the inequity either by distorting inputs and/or outcomes psychologically, by directly altering inputs and/or outputs, or by quitting the organization.

Expectancy Theory of Motivation

The expectancy theory was proposed by Victor Vroom of Yale School of Management in 1964. Vroom stresses and focuses on outcomes, and not on needs unlike Maslow and Herzberg. The theory states that the intensity of a tendency to perform in a particular manner is dependent on the intensity of an expectation that the performance will be followed by a definite outcome and on the appeal of the outcome to the individual. The Expectancy *theory* states that employee's motivation is an outcome of how much an individual wants a reward (Valence), the assessment that the likelihood that the effort will lead to expected performance (Expectancy) and the belief that the performance will lead to reward (Instrumentality). In short, *Valence* is the significance associated by an individual about the expected outcome. It is an expected and not the actual satisfaction that an employee expects to receive after achieving the goals. *Expectancy* is the faith that better efforts will result in better performance. Expectancy is influenced by factors such as possession of appropriate skills for performing the job, availability of right resources, availability of crucial information and getting the required support for completing the job.

Instrumentality is the faith that if you perform well, then a valid outcome will be there. Instrumentality is affected by factors such as believe in the people who decide who receives what outcome, the simplicity of the process deciding who gets what outcome, and clarity of relationship between performance and outcomes. Thus, the expectancy theory concentrates on the following three relationships:

- *Effort-performance relationship:* What is the likelihood that the individual's effort be recognized in his performance appraisal?

- *Performance-reward relationship:* It talks about the extent to which the employee believes that getting a good performance appraisal leads to organizational rewards.

— *Rewards-personal goals relationship:* It is all about the attractiveness or appeal of the potential reward to the individual.

Vroom was of view that employees consciously decide whether to perform or not at the job. This decision solely depended on the employee's motivation level which in turn depends on three factors of expectancy, valence and instrumentality.

Advantages of the Expectancy Theory

— It is based on self-interest individual who want to achieve maximum satisfaction and who wants to minimize dissatisfaction.
— This theory stresses upon the expectations and perception; what is real and actual is immaterial.
— It emphasizes on rewards or pay-offs.
— It focuses on psychological extravagance where final objective of individual is to attain maximum pleasure and least pain.

Limitations of the Expectancy Theory

— The expectancy theory seems to be idealistic because quite a few individuals perceive high degree correlation between performance and rewards.
— The application of this theory is limited as reward is not directly correlated with performance in many organizations. It is related to other parameters also such as position, effort, responsibility, education, etc.

Implications of the Expectancy Theory

— The managers can correlate the preferred outcomes to the aimed performance levels.

— The managers must ensure that the employees can achieve the aimed performance levels.

— The deserving employees must be rewarded for their exceptional performance.

— The reward system must be fair and just in an organization.

— Organizations must design interesting, dynamic and challenging jobs.

— The employee's motivation level should be continually assessed through various techniques such as questionnaire, personal interviews, etc.

3

PRINCIPLES OF MOTIVATION

Motivation seems to be a simple function of management in books, but in practice it is more challenging. The reasons for motivation being challenging job are as follows:

— One of the main reasons of motivation being a challenging job is due to the changing workforce. The employees become a part of their organization with various needs and expectations. Different employees have different beliefs, attitudes, values, backgrounds and thinking. But all the organizations are not aware of the diversity in their workforce and thus are not aware and clear about different ways of motivating their diverse workforce.

— Employees motives cannot be seen, they can only be presumed. Suppose, there are two employees in a team showing varying performance despite being of same age group, having same educational qualifications and same work experience. The reason being what motivates one employee may not seem motivating to other.

— Motivation of employees becomes challenging especially when the organizations have considerably changed the job role of the employees, or have lessened the hierarchy levels of hierarchy, or have chucked out a significant number of employees in the name of down-sizing or right-sizing. Certain firms have chosen to hire and fire and paying for performance strategies nearly giving up motivational efforts. These strategies are unsuccessful in making an individual overreach himself.

— The vigorous nature of needs also pose challenge to a manager in motivating his subordinates. This is because an employee at a certain point of time has diverse needs and expectations. Also, these needs and expectations keep on changing and might also clash with each other. For instance—the employees who spend extra time at work for meeting their needs for accomplishment might discover that the extra time spent by them clash with their social neds and with the need for affiliation.

A man, woman or child is motivated when he or she *wants* to do something. Motivation covers all the reasons which cause a person to act, including negative ones like fear along with the more positive motives, such as money, promotion or recognition. The extent to which you can motivate anyone else is limited, for 50 per cent of the cards are, so to speak, in their hands. You can provide motives or incentives in one way or another; you can offer rewards or issue threats; you can attempt to persuade. All these actual or potential influences may have an effect, for remember that 50 per cent of a person's motivation stems from the environment. If you are a leader, then you are a key factor in the environment of those who work for you. But your power is limited. As the proverb says, 'You can take a horse to water, but you cannot make him drink.'

The principles or rules of motivation are described below. How you apply them will clearly depend upon the situation. But they stand as pillars of encouragement, both inviting you to take up your responsibility as a leader for inspiring others and pointing you in the right direction.

1. BE MOTIVATED YOURSELF

The first and golden rule of motivation is that you will never inspire others unless you are inspired yourself. Only a motivated leader motivates others. Example is the great seducer. It is so simple and so obvious, isn't it? But why is it so neglected in management today? Enthusiasm inspires, especially when combined with trust. Its key importance can perhaps best be seen by considering its opposites. What impression would we make as leaders if we were apathetic, stolid, halfhearted, indifferent and uninterested? Enthusiasm is infectious; and enthusiasts are usually competent too, since they believe in and like what they are doing. One of the world's first philosopher-consultants, Confucius, was once called in by a Chinese feudal king to check the corruption and theft which was rife in his domain. The fact that both the king and his court indulged in these practices, and that others were taking their cue from them, soon became apparent to Confucius, and he simply pointed out to his client the motivating influence—for good or ill—of example. 'If you did not steal yourself,' he said, 'even if you rewarded men with gold to steal they would not do it.' Before you criticize others for lack of motivation ask yourself if your own enthusiasm for and commitment to the task in hand is sincere, visible and tangible. Have you expressed it in deeds as well as words? Are you setting a good example? For motivation is caught, not taught.

2. SELECT PEOPLE WHO ARE HIGHLY MOTIVATED

Since it is hard to motivate people who are not already motivated it makes sense to select those who already are.

It is true that in the coldest flint there is hot fire, but you may lack the skill to release such hidden sparks. Bunyan added that 'great grace and small gifts are better than great gifts and no grace', which can be translated here to mean that when you select someone for a job a high motivation and modest talent is to be preferred to considerable talent but little or no evidence of motivation.

Given the absence of any reliable psychological tests to measure motivation, managers are thrown back on their judgement. Some useful tips for interviewers are:

— Remember that someone at an interview is trying to influence or motivate you to give them the job. Some people find it easy to *act* as if they are highly motivated or enthusiastic for an hour during an interview. Others, who may be very motivated, may come across as 'laid back'.

— By their fruits you shall know them. Look for evidence in what they have done. What someone wishes to do he or she will find a way of doing. Has persistence and perseverance—evidences of high motivation—ever been shown? Ask the referees who know him or her well.

— Describe several work situations that require high motivation and ask the applicant how he or she would react.

3. TREAT EACH PERSON AS AN INDIVIDUAL

Unless you ask a person what motivates them—what they want—you will not know. We are all individuals. What motivates one person in the team may not motivate another. Enter into some sort of dialogue with each individual member of the group. A wise leader in an organization always remembers that a whole bushel of wheat is made up of single grains. By listening to individuals, giving them an opportunity to express their hopes and fears, the leader is also showing true care. The intention, however, must be to help if possible and not to manipulate. 'You would play upon me... You would seek to know my stops... You would pluck out the heart of my mystery'. That is cynical manipulation, as unmasked in Shakespeare's words.

Leadership stands in sharp contrast to such person-management. Sir John Smythe VC wrote,

> A good leader is someone whom people will follow through thick and thin, in good times and bad, because they have confidence in him as a person, his ability and his knowledge of the job, and because *they know they matter to him.*

4. SET REALISTIC AND CHALLENGING TARGETS

'There is no inspiration in the ideals of plenty and stability,' wrote John Lancaster Spalding. People are capable of transcending self in the pursuit of high and demanding ideals.Most people reveal this capacity in the way they respond better to a challenge. There is a fine balance here. If objectives are totally unrealistic they will demotivate people: if they are too easy to attain, on the other hand, they are also uninspiring. As a leader you have to get the balance right. 'It is not enough to do our best,' said Winston Churchill. 'Sometimes we have to do what is required.'

It is essential to agree targets or objectives with those who have to carry them out. For the principle is true that the more we share decisions which affect working lives, the more we are motivated to carry them out. If the person accepts that the objective is both realistic and desirable or important, then he or she will start drawing upon their 50 per cent of the motivational equation.

5. REMEMBER THAT PROGRESS MOTIVATES

We are motivated not simply by individual needs but also by needs emanating from the common task. We want to finish what we are doing. The more significant the task, the stronger is the need to complete it satisfactorily. John Wesley called it 'the lust to finish'. It is a sound principle that progress motivates. If people know that they are moving forwards it leads them to increase their efforts. We invest more in success. Therefore it is important to ensure that people receive proper feedback. Feedback is defined in *Webster's Dictionary* as 'the return to the input of a part of the output of a machine, system or process'. Without feedback people will not know if they are moving in the right direction at the right speed. Conversely, feedback on relative lack of progress also motivates. For it concentrates minds on what must be done if success is to be yet achieved. If you confront people with the realities of their situation in this way, then the 'law of the situation' will do the work of motivation for you.

6. CREATE A MOTIVATING ENVIRONMENT

Although you have limited power to motivate others you can do a great deal to create an environment which they will find motivating. Most of us have experienced the flip-side of such an environment: one that reduces motivation. A restrictive organizational culture, which overemphasizes controls and reduces people to passive roles, coupled with an unpredictable and irascible superior who tells off people in public, is hardly likely to bring out the best in human nature. It is important that Herzberg's 'hygiene' factors are properly catered for. The physical and psychological well-being of people has to have a top priority. Only introduce control systems where necessary, for over-controlling does reduce motivation. Double-check that people have a proper input into the decisions that affect their working lives, especially when any substantial change is involved. Keep units or sub-units as small as possible, for large organizations tend to become bureaucratic and demotivational if they lack inspired leaders.

Lastly, pay attention to job design. Repetitive work can become boring if uninterrupted, so introduce as much variety as possible. Let people work on something they can recognize as their own product, for people find real autonomy motivates them. Ensure that the person doing the job understands its impact on others, so that they see the significance of it. That is vital, especially if you want people to be so involved that they contribute new ideas and help forward the essential process of innovation.

7. PROVIDE FAIR REWARDS

A lynx chasing a snow rabbit will only chase it for about 200 metres, then it gives up. For the food gained if the prey was caught will not replace the energy lost in the pursuit. Working on the same unconscious principle, it will chase a deer for longer. All work implies this element of balancing what we give with what we expect to receive. Fairness or justice means that the return should be equivalent in value to the contribution. Performance ought to be linked to rewards, just as promotion should be related to merit. The former— getting financial rewards fair—is easier said than done in many work situations. But the principle is still important and ways of applying it have to be found. Justinian wrote that 'Justice is the constant and unceasing will to give everyone his right or due.' That genuine and sustained intention is expected from any leader who has discretion over the distribution of rewards. The principle has to be applied with especial care over monetary remunerations, for if fairness is not perceived there it can breed a lack of motivation and low morale. When remuneration is poor, workers put less effort into their jobs. Money is a key incentive. Therefore proper job evaluation schemes, involving a representative group of work people in the judgements about the financial worth of jobs, are vitally important. There are, of course, other rewards we gain from working, as Maslow's hierarchy of needs illustrates. Opportunities for professional development and personal growth are especially valuable to good people. But money has a strategic importance for most people, not least as a measure of recognition for the significance of their contributions. As the means of exchange and as a store of wealth, money is probably the most useful material reward you can give.

8. GIVE RECOGNITION

Recognition is often an even more powerful motivator. Money anyway often means more to people as a tangible symbol of recognition than as the wherewithal to buy more material goods. This thirst for recognition is universal. In gifted people it amounts to a desire for fame or glory For example, Isambard Brunel could write in his diary: 'My self-conceit and love of glory, or rather approbation, vie with each other which shall govern me.' As a leader you can give recognition and show appreciation in a variety of ways. A sincere 'well done' or 'thank you' can work wonders for a person's morale.

4

POWER OF MOTIVATION

To motivate others is the most important of management tasks. It comprises the abilities to communicate, to set an example, to challenge, to encourage, to obtain feedback, to involve, to delegate, to develop and train, to inform, to brief and to provide a just reward. Motivation seems to provoke the response that everybody wants it but they are not quite sure what it is. We see in various job advertisements that the candidate must be self-motivated.

Human beings, as we know, are natural goal seekers and it seems that all the amazing achievements in the world come from highly motivated individuals. We all live in a world of increasing complexity with incredible technology at our command. The developments of information technology, microchips, the internet and the progress in electronic data pro cessing and creativity fields are mind blowing. Yet the real world in which we all work is, of course, a people's world. Parents produce children, those children go through their educational years and then move on to develop their own career. They in turn build relationships, get married and again children are produced. And so the cycle perpetuates itself. Very few of us during our educational years had much, if any, instruction on ourselves, communication, people or motivation.

Virtually everybody can motivate themselves and should be motivating somebody else.

If you understand what motivates people, you have at your command the most powerful tool for dealing with them. Motivation appears to be a general requirement. Everybody wants more motivation, but they're not quite sure what it is. The individual would say they would like to be more motivated. The manager or the leader would like to have a more motivated team or group, and the employer wishes to employ a motivated person. In fact, the employer's demands are even greater in that the person they need should be self-motivated.

Motivation and power are so closely linked that one can say there is power in a motivated person. You may recall that extraordinary story of the 5'4" mother weighing some nine stone who had a terrible car accident with her baby son on board. The car ended up on its side with the child trapped underneath. The mother was fortunately thrown clear and unhurt. When the rescue services arrived, they found the mother cradling her child in her arms, also unhurt. They were taken to hospital for a complete check-up, where it was discovered that the vertebrae in the mother's back had been crushed. Apparently, what had happened was that she had lifted the car, removed the child with her feet and, in the process, damaged her back. There was no known way under normal circumstance that the mother could have lifted the vehicle. She did not have the physique, the strength or the muscle power. But she did have the power of motivation.

Hope is therefore a criterion for people to be motivated. It is the cause for the effect—the fuel that drives the engine. Without hope, no person could ever be motivated. Historically, management was more about managing muscle than brain. It was the responsibility of the managers to think, to organize, to plan and then to convey clear instructions for their employees to carry out the tasks without deviation, hesitation or repetition. Nowadays, very little muscle is employed. What managers do have the responsibility for is the management of other people's brains, and probably one of their biggest frustrations is the often-voiced frustration 'Why didn't you think?'

Therefore, if you are hiring a person's brain, the old-fashioned management techniques really are redundant and have to be replaced by leadership, skills, behaviour and demonstration.

MOTIVATION AND MANIPULATION

Let us begin by distinguishing the difference from the management viewpoint between motivation and manipulation.

Manipulation seems to be getting somebody to do something because you want them to do it; whereas motivation is getting somebody to do some thing because they want to do it. And there is the difference.

For far too long in the recent history of business in the world, management has operated under a manipulative regime and nations have suffered from poor–and in many cases busy–management.

The world in which we work is a people's world, yet still in many organizations people are promoted into a management or leadership role because they are good at another job or task. Very rarely are people trained on how to manage others. Because they were good or effective in some other role, they are now expected by their peers to assume the title of manager and, by some God-given right, to know automatically how to motivate, communicate with and manage others.

And so the cycle perpetuates itself because many of these managers follow the manipulative style of their predecessors.

Sure, manipulation does work. But it doesn't last and creates mistrust, leading to a 'them and us' situation.

A manipulative style of people management does not create the ideal where managers and their staff all pull together in the same direction to achieve their shared goals.

It is rather naive to encourage self-motivated people to attend an interview but expect the successful candidate to react kindly to manipulation when employed.

Motivation is getting somebody to do something because they want to do it. This also applies to you and — if we really want to do something, we will be more motivated; and if we really don't want to do something, we will lack self-motivation.

It is probably helpful to accept and understand the pain and pleasure principle. We, like the rest of the animal world, will do what we can to avoid pain. There is, of course, the natural instinct to avoid any likelihood of experiencing physical pain. Equally, we have a natural instinct to avoid any form of mental discomfort. Instances of this instinct include the reaction when faced with an unpleasant task such as the difficult phone call, the household chore, the meeting that could be confrontational, opening the bills, exercising in order to keep fit and giving up smoking. On the other hand, we will go to great lengths in quest to seek pleasure or perceived pleasure, which in some cases is short lived — eating too much, drinking too much. On the positive side, the drive for pleasure is, of course, crucial to achievement, as we will see when we look at goal achievement in more detail. The achievers of this world manage to get the balance of the pain and pleasure principle right. Many non-achievers procrastinate by putting off doing the important or nasty job, and in many cases do not expose themselves to any position where pain could be a possibility—unprepared to ever take a risk.

In putting motivation into some perspective we must also distinguish the difference between *attitude motivation* and *incentive motivation.*

We all know of the 'carrot and stick' style of motivation. And as this is a view that many people still have of motivation, let us distinguish the difference between the two different kinds listed above.

ATTITUDE MOTIVATION

Attitude motivation is how people think and feel. It is their self-confidence, their belief in themselves, their attitude to life—be it positive or negative. It is how they feel about the future and how they react to the past. All of us from time to time have to make sure that we have the right attitude—but more about that later.

GOOD ENVIRONMENT

As we go through the techniques of building motivation and putting the subject into its proper perspective, it is essential to understand that for an individual, a team or group of people, motivation can only be effective in the right environment. For example, a manager may attempt to motivate a team of people by introducing a competition or incentive programme, which may well have been properly constructed, but if the environment in which that team is operating is not conducive to a harmonious relationship, there is backbiting, mistrust or an unhappy atmosphere, any incentive or attempted motivational approach will be ineffective.

To be an effective manager and motivator of others, one must have or develop leadership skills. This is common sense, but nevertheless worth repeating. When the leaders are leading, the followers will follow. Of course, people copy their peers and one cannot divorce leadership styles from motivational results. 'Set a good example', leaders have been told since the beginning of time.

MOTIVATED PERSON

Let's now create an image of a motivated person. A motivated person will surely have a smart outward appearance; their hair will look as though it has been taken care of, clothes will be pressed and freshly laundered, shoes clean. The outward appearance is therefore of somebody who cares about themself. One should also notice the way people walk.

Secondly, body language will convey a person's enthusiasm. A smiling face, sparking eyes and a positive facial expression can certainly convey an individual's motivation.

Students of body language claim that in this part of Europe, we are able to communicate with approximately 40,000 words and sounds, though on a day-to-day basis we habitually use just 4,000. On the other hand, body language signals conveyed from the face alone can number some 15,000. We know that the majority of people can control what they say. So whenever body language is in conflict with the spoken word due to the sheer number of body language signals, the body language will almost certainly be conveying the correct information.

So somebody saying that they actually feel fine, but with a pained facial expression or stooped shoulders that clearly shows the opposite, can be studied, and their true feelings can be deduced.

Finally, how does a motivated person communicate? With enthusiasm. A motivated person talks about the future, what they are doing or planning to do. The past is used as experience to recognize and turn opportunities into success. The motivated person, therefore, has a zest for life and is a pleasure to be with.

And above everything else, a motivated person is what one could easily describe as a positive person. That is, showing the characteristics of an attitude that is:

— positive;

— motivated by a purpose;

— expecting to succeed.

This in turn generates energy. Motivated people seem to have an abundance of this. You have heard the expression: 'If you want something done, ask a busy person.'

❖❖❖

5

MOTIVATIONAL LEADERSHIP

Leadership and motivation are like brother and sister. It is difficult to think of a leader who does not motivate others. But leadership embraces more than motivation.

Motivation is a goal-oriented characteristic that helps a person achieve his objectives. It pushes an individual to work hard at achieving his or her goals. An executive must have the right leadership traits to influence motivation. However, there is no specific blueprint for motivation. As a leader, one should keep an open perspective on human nature. Knowing different needs of subordinates will certainly make the decision-making process easier.

Both an employee as well as manager must possess leadership and motivational traits. An effective leader must have a thorough knowledge of motivational factors for others. He must understand the basic needs of employees, peers and his superiors. Leadership is used as a means of motivating others.

Remember, "to become an efficient leader, you must be self-motivated". You must know your identity, your needs and you must have a strong urge to do anything to achieve your goals. Once you are self-motivated, only then you can motivate others to achieve their goals and to harmonize their personal goals with the common goals of the organization.

Functional leadership training was first developed at the Royal Military Academy (Sandhurst) of United Kingdom, as part of a programme introducing young officers to the responsibilities of leadership. When transposed into industry and commerce it was renamed Action-Centred Leadership (ACL). Initially, the core content of ACL remained much the same as the original Sandhurst version, though the practical exercises and case studies where changed.

Working groups resemble individuals in that although they are always unique (each develops its own 'group personality') yet they share, as do individuals, certain common 'needs'. There are three areas of need present in such groups. Two of these are the properties of the group as a whole, namely *the need to accomplish the common tasks* and *the need to be maintained as a cohesive social unity*. The third area is constituted by the sum of the *individual needs* of group members.

INDIVIDUAL NEEDS AND MOTIVATION

This area of need present in the corporate life inheres in the individual members rather than in the group itself. To the latter they bring a variety of needs—physical, social, intellectual and spiritual—which may or may not be met by participating in the activity of the group. Probably physical needs first drew men together in working groups: the primitive hunter could take away from the slain elephant a hunk of meat and a piece of hide for his own family. Nowadays the means for satisfying these basic needs of food, shelter and protection are received in money rather than in kind, but the principle remains the same. There are, however, other needs less tangible or conscious even to their possessors which the social interaction of working together in groups may or may not fulfil. These tend to merge into one another, and they cannot be isolated with any precision, but the followinf diagram indicate their character.

Physiological	Safety	Social	Esteem	Self-actualization
				Growth
			Self-respect	
		Belonging	Status	
	Security	Social activities	Recognition	Personal
Hunger	Protection from danger			
Thirst		Love		development
Sleep				Accomplishment

Priority of needs

These need spring from the depths of common life as human beings. Underlying them all is the fact that people need one another, not just to survive but to achieve and develop personality. This growth occurs in a whole range of social activity—friendship, marriage, neighbourhood— but inevitably work groups are extremely important because so many people spend so much of their waking time in them.

Professor Frederick Herzberg has dichotomized the list by suggesting that the factors which make people experience satisfaction in their work situation are not the reverse of those which make them dissatisfied. The latter is caused by deficiencies in the environment or context of the job; in contrast, job satisfaction rests upon the content of the work and the opportunities it presents for achievement, recognition, professional development, and personal growth.

Interaction of Needs

The first major point is that these three areas of need influence one another for better or worse. For example, if a group fails in its task this will intensify the disintegrative tendencies present in the group and produce a diminished satisfaction for its individual members. If there is a lack of unity or harmonious relationships in the group this will affect performance on the job and also individual needs. And obviously an individual who feels frustrated and unhappy in a particular work environment will not make his or her maximum contribution to either the common task or to the life of the group. Conversely, achievement in terms of a common aim tends to build a sense of group identity—the 'we-feeling', as some have called it. The moment of victory closes the psychological gaps between people: morale rises naturally. Good internal communications and a developed team spirit based upon past successes make a group much more likely to do well in its task area, and incidentally provide a more satisfactory climate for the individual. Lastly, an individual whose needs are recognized and who feels that he or she can make a characteristic and worthwhile contribution both to the task and the group will tend to produce good fruits in both these areas.

We can illustrate these interrelations with a simple model:

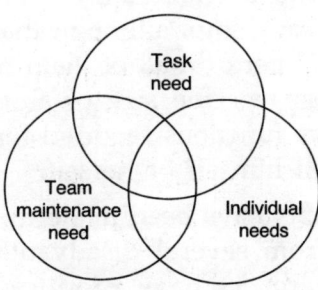

Interaction of needs

If you place a coin over the 'Task' circle it will immediately cover segments of the other two circles as well. In other words, lack of task or failure to achieve it will affect both team maintenance, e.g. increasing disruptive tendencies, and also the area of individual needs, lowering member satisfaction within the group. Move the coin on to the 'Team' circle, and again the impact of a near-complete lack of relationships in the group on both task and individual needs may be seen at a glance. Conversely, when a group achieves its task the degree of group cohesiveness and enjoyment or membership should go up. Morale, both corporate and individual, will be higher. And if the members of a group happen to get on extremely well together and find that they can work closely as a team, this will increase their work performance and also meet some important needs which individuals bring with them into the common life.

These three interlocking circles therefore illustrate the general point that each area of need exerts an influence upon the other two: they do not form watertight compartments.

LEADERSHIP FUNCTIONS

In order for the needs in these areas to be met in any group or organization certain functions have to be performed. According to this integrated theory the provision of these necessary functions is the responsibility of leadership, although that does not imply that the leader will perform all of them himself or herself. Indeed, in groups over the size of about five members there are too many functions required for any one person to supply them all himself or herself.

Various attempts have been made to list the functions but they suffer from several disadvantages. In the first place, some researchers have produced three separate lists, one for each area. The difference between 'Task' and 'Team Maintenance' is always in danger of yawning into a dichotomy. The value of the three overlapping circles is that they emphasize the essential unity of leadership: a single action can be multi-functional in that it touches all three areas. The distinction between the circles should not therefore be pressed too far, and separate lists favour that unfortunate tendency. Secondly, many of the lists reflect the 'group dynamics laboratory' situation too much. Thirdly, it is rather artificial to categorize the response of leaders to individual needs. It is sufficient to recognize that effective leaders are aware of this dimension, and respond in appropriate ways with understanding. Such action might range from changing the content of an individual's job or role, along the lines advocated by Professor Herzberg, to a promotion or a word of encouragement. It is perhaps best to work out a single list of leadership functions within the context of a given working situation, so that the subheadings can have the stamp of reality upon them. But there is general agreement upon the essentials, and to illustrate some of these major functions meeting the three interacting areas of need, a list originally worked out, is given below, which has been the basis for numerous adaptations in industry and other fields:

1. *Planning*
   - Seeking all available information.
   - Defining group task, purpose or goal.
   - Making a workable plan (in right decision-making framework).

2. *Initiating* e.g. briefing group on the aims and the plan.
   - Explaining why aim or plan is necessary.
   - Allocating tasks to group members.

      — Setting group standards.

3. *Controlling*

      — Maintaining group standards.

      — Influencing tempo.

      — Ensuring all actions are taken towards objectives.

      — Keeping discussion relevant.

      — Prodding group to action/decision.

4. *Supporting*

      — Expressing acceptance of people and their contribution.

      — Encouraging group/individuals.

      — Disciplining group/individuals.

      — Creating team spirit.

      — Relieving tension with humour.

      — Reconciling disagreements or getting others to explore them.

5. *Informing*

      — Clarifying task and plan.

      — Giving new information to the group, i.e. keeping them 'in the picture'.

      — Receiving information from group.

      — Summarizing suggestions and ideas coherently.

6. *Evaluating*

      — Checking feasibility of an idea.

      — Testing consequences of a proposed solution.

      — Evaluating group performance.

      — Helping the group to evaluate its own performance against standards.

SHARING DECISIONS

Without forgetting the broader opportunities open to members for supplementing the work of leadership in all three areas described above, it is especially useful to examine specifically the extent to which the leader should share with others the general function of decision-making, the core of such more definite functions as setting objectives and planning. In an invaluable diagram R Tannenbaum and W H Schmidt plotted the possibilities of participation. The diagram can be compared to a cake: at one end the leader has virtually all of it, and at the other the group has the lion's share. In terms of a transaction between a leader and an individual follower the continuum also illustrates the degrees of delegation that are possible in the context of a given decision.

There is much to be said for moving as far to the right of the continuum as possible, for the more that people share in decisions which directly affect them the more they are motivated to carry them out—provided they trust the integrity of the leader who is inviting them to participate in the decision. Yet factors in the situation and the *group* will naturally limit the extent to which the right-hand edge of the continuum can be approached. Other limiting factors may be present in the personality of the leader or the value system and philosophy of a particular organization, factors which cannot be described as natural or intrinsic in the same way as the situational or group constraints.

There are some groups and organizations whose characteristic working situations (as contrasted to the actual ones they may be in for 90 per cent of their time) are essentially crisis ones, where by definition time is short for decisions and the matter of life or death rests upon prompt decisions from one man, e.g. operating theatre teams, fire brigades, police forces, airline crews and military organizations. Yet such groups are not always in crisis situations, and for training purposes, if for no other reason, they need to explore the decision-making scale. Moreover, although it is not always possible to share decisions over ends (i.e. goals, objectives, aims or purpose) it is usually possible to involve others more or less fully in means (i.e. methods, techniques, conditions, and plans). Rather than engaging in the fruitless attempt to establish a particular spot or 'style' on the scale which is 'best' should see the continuum as a sliding scale, or as a thermometer marked with boiling and freezing points. Where the latter points fall on the scale will depend upon the characteristic working situation of the group or organization. There will be a difference, for example, between an earth-shifting gang of labourers constructing a motorway and a research group in an electronics or chemical firm.

ACTION-CENTRED LEADERSHIP

The model at the core of Action-Centred Leadership (ACL)—the three overlapping circles of Task, Team and Individual -has become one of the most widely taught concepts in the world. Its simplicity, coupled with its proven track record as a basis for leadership training courses, commends it to management developers. Many now use it to integrate a number of other concepts, ideas and practices which can be grouped under the heading of 'the human side of enterprise'. The ACL model is now acknowledged to be the equivalent in this field to Einstein's General Theory of Relativity in physics. For it does identify the three main forces at work in working groups and organizations, and it charts their main interrelationships with a degree of predictive accuracy.

This simplicity, however, is deceptive. True simplicity is different from the simplistic or superficial. Einstein's words warn us against such a reduction: 'Everything should be made as simple as possible, but not more simple' he once said. Many books which reproduce the three circles, and many organizations that purport to teach ACL, do tend to pick out the three-circles diagram because it is so distinctive. But they then skate over, or leave out altogether, other ingredients in the original ACL complex of ideas which is essential. This can lead to distortion. Indeed the originality of ACL lay not in its parts but in their integration into a whole which is more than their parts and in the application of them to training. By being brought into a new relation with one another those parts have undergone varying degrees of transformation, which is inevitable in any creative work.

Qualities Approach

The qualities approach, for example, was universally unpopular after the Second World War among management theorists and social psychologists. The idea that leadership might characterize one person rather than another, not least because he or she possessed leadership qualities, was then deeply unfashionable among social scientists for cultural reasons. The ACL general theory was virtually unique in those days in retaining it as a contributory source to understanding of leadership. The false assumptions latent in the understanding of leadership were indeed challenged by a few individuals, notably William H Whyte in *The Organizational Man*. A decade later A H Maslow visited several organizations in California and commented:

> What I smell here is again some of the democratic dogma and piety in which all people are equal and in which the conception of a factually strong person or natural leader or dominant person or superior intellect or superior decisiveness or whatever is bypassed because it makes everybody uncomfortable

and because it seems to contradict the democratic philosophy.

It took more than another decade before behavioural scientists, such as Warren Bennis and Bernard Bass, backtracked to the qualities approach. Then a spate of books on leadership poured from the presses discussing the qualities required in leaders. In a sense this change of heart was market-led. What happened? Reeling under fierce competition from Japanese companies, corporate United States began to look for better leadership from their chief executives. In original ACL theory the first principle about the qualities of leaders suggests that they tend to possess the qualities expected or admired in their work groups. Physical courage, for example, does not make you into a military leader, but you cannot be one without it. A large part of the popularity of President Reagan of United States, to give a second example, stemmed from the fact that many Americans saw him as personifying the core characteristics and values. This point does suggest a powerful link between leadership and given work situations, and may help to explain why the transfer of leadership from one field to another is often so difficult.

The British tradition on leadership has always emphasized the moral qualities of a good leader, such as moral courage and integrity. The early researchers compared some of the lists of qualities—such as initiative, perseverance, courage—which emerged from empirical research on leadership in order to see which words appeared on all or most lists. They found little or no agreement. For example, one classic survey of 20 experimental studies revealed that only 5 per cent of the leadership qualities examined were common to four or more studies. High intelligence came top; it appeared in 10 lists, followed by initiative which was mentioned in six of them. As there are some 17,000 words in the

English language relating to personality and character there seemed to be plenty of choice and ample margin for error. These researchers were in fact victims of what philosophers have called the *word-concept fallacy*. Two words—such as *perseverance* and *persistence*—may be different, but they belong to the same family of meaning, the same concept. The researchers should have been fishing with wider meshed nets. For they should have been seeking clusters of meanings or concepts.

It is true that a different message emanated from Machiavelli in the 16th century, but this godless Italian doctrine was never accepted into the mainstream of the Western tradition concerning leadership. The moral qualities approach—based upon Aristotle's four virtues: justice, prudence, fortitude and temperance—was far too deep-seated. Even in *The Path to Leadership* Field-Marshall Lord Montgomery could refer with approval to them. For this reason leaders in the Western culture who pursue immoral ends, or employ cynical, Machiavellian manipulation to achieve their ends, are unlikely to enjoy more than a brief success. Hitler did not last.

Situational Approach

The situational approach, or contingency theory as it is now called, enjoyed a vogue in the 1960s mainly as a result of the work of Professor F. E. Fiedler of the University of Illinois and his associates. They studied the extent to which leadership veered towards the two poles of 'task oriented' and 'considerate' and tried to predict the circumstances in which one of these leadership 'styles' would be more effective than the other. Factors such as group composition, the degree of structuring in the task, and the 'position power' of the leader came into play. Fiedler believed that: 'We can improve the effectiveness of leadership by accurate diagnosis of the group-task situation and by altering the leader's work environment.' Like so many ideas and models, despite much revised work on the variables in the situation, Fiedler's work has not stood the test of time. It is now of little interest, except to specialists in the history of psychological research. But of course the idea that the influence of the situation pervades leadership is by no means out of date. ACL theory has always made four points under the heading of the Situational Approach:

— Situations are partly constant and partly variable. For example, working in a bank has a continuity and a uniqueness compared with, say, working in a hospital. This is true of all fields, for they are all unique. But there has been much change in banking (as in all other fields). So it's a partly constant, partly changing situation.

— Leaders personify or exemplify (or should do so) the qualities expected or required in their working groups. This principle clearly links leadership to particular working situations.

— The situational approach highlights the importance of *knowledge* in leadership. There are three forms of authority in human affairs: the authorities of position, knowledge and personality. The latter in its extreme form is what is correctly called 'charisma'. Knowledge is especially important. As the proverb says, 'Authority flows to him who knows.'

— Some people, however, who acquire considerable technical or professional knowledge, and are specialists in a particular kind of work, are not perceived by their colleagues or subordinates as leaders. In other words, there is more to leadership than technical knowledge. It is this more general or transferable aspect that the Qualities Approach attempted—with only partial success—to analyse and define.

It's a question of level really. At the team leadership level, technical or professional knowledge is clearly very important.

Nobody is going to respect a leader who manifestly does not know what he or she is talking about. The 'leader' of an orchestra, for example, must be able to play the violin and lead the strings. At the *operational* and *strategic* levels of leadership, where the more general kinds of leadership knowledge become more important, the degree of technical or specialist knowledge required is smaller although none the less important. The conductor of an orchestra, to continue that example, does not have to be a good instrumentalist.

Transfer within a general field, such as industry or commerce, must be contrasted to transfer *between* general fields, such as military to politics, or industry to hospitals. Obviously the former is relatively more easy. A chief executive moving from company to company takes with him or her a transferable cluster of leadership skills—including decision-making and communication know-how—and also a transferrable cluster of business abilities, notably in finance and marketing. All that remains to be learnt is the particular technology involved in the product or service. What matters now is speed of learning.

A good strategic leader will soon acquire all that he or she needs to know. Lack of background knowledge can be turned into an advantage in so far as it keeps you out of the engine room when you should be on the bridge. Getting involved unnecessarily in detail is one of the failings of those who rise to the top in their own fields.

Individual Needs

Maslow did not himself actually use a diagram to illustrate his hierarchy of needs. The familiar model in the shape of a pyramid (digram A below) must therefore have been a later addition, but it is now commonplace in textbooks on management. Unfortunately this way of presenting Maslow's hierarchy makes it look as if the greatest needs are in the lower ranges, and that they narrow in size as you progress up the pyramid. But physiological needs, for example, are limited: you can only eat so many meals a day. In fact there are fewer limitations the further up you go. Therefore, it you persist with the pyramid model, it makes more sense to invert it thus diagram B.

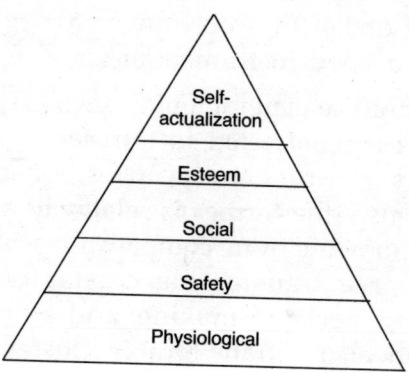

(A) The pyramid model of human needs

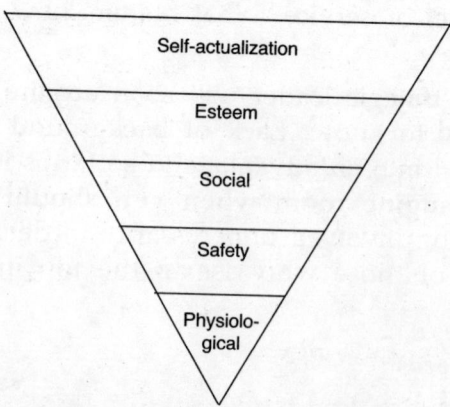

(B) Inverted pyramid of human needs

Be that as it may, the visual difficulties of the pyramid in its original form are obviated if the diagram of boxes in ascending size is used. It has always seemed to the better way of representing Maslow's hierarchy of needs.

LEADERSHIP AND MANAGEMENT FUNCTIONS

Henri Fayol, who was born in 1841, was a French mining engineer and became the director of a large group of coal pits before retiring in 1918. He published *General and Industrial Administration* two years earlier, but the first English translation of it did not appear until 1949. In it Fayol divided the activities of an industrial company into six main groups:

1. *Technical*—production, manufacture, adaptation.
2. *Commercial*—buying, selling, exchange.
3. *Financial*—search for an optimum use of capital.
4. *Security*—protection of property and people.
5. *Accounting*—stocktaking, balance sheet, costs, statistics.
6. *Administration*—forecasting and planning, organizing, commanding, co-ordinating and controlling.

Fayol defined the function of command as 'getting the organization going' and he gives some examples of what it means in practice. A person in command should:

— Have a thorough knowledge of employees.
— Eliminate the incompetent.
— Be well versed in the agreements binding the business and its employees.
— Set a good example.
— Conduct periodic audits of the organization and use summarized charts to further this review.

— Bring together his chief assistants by means of conferences at which unity of direction and focusing of effort are provided for.

— Not become engrossed in detail.

— Aim at making unity, energy, initiative and loyalty prevail among all employees.

Fayol's analysis of managing in terms of functions has been subjected to much critical discussion. L. F. Urwick, an early British exponent of Fayol's theory, in his *The Elements of Administration*, substituted the English word readership' for Fayol's 'command'. The ACL general theory provides a natural framework for Fayol's pioneering work. In it Fayol's list of functions could be developed in such a way as to ensure that all three areas of need—task, team or group, and individual—are met. It points out that a classic function such as *planning*, which may seem to be merely a task function, in fact influences both the other areas of need for good or ill. Moreover, Fayol is brought up to date by the addition of some more general functions in the team-building and team maintenance area, as well as functional responses to the individual needs circle.

Decision-Making Continuum

The Tannenbaum and Schmidt continuum, which first appeared in the *Harvard Business Review*, was always integral to the ACL general theory. It has a direct link with motivation for the reason given, namely that *the more that people share in a decision which affects their working life the more they tend to be motivated to carry it out*. This is a fundamental principle in motivation. The Tannenbaum and Schmidt continuum was the subject of academic research which has greatly enhanced its standing.

People do expect leaders to be consistent in personality and character, yet flexible when it comes to decision-making. So that an effective leader, it has been shown, will make decisions on different points of the continuum during a single working day and be right each time. For he or she will be taking into account—consciously or subconsciously—such factors as the knowledge, motivation and experience of the group or individual concerned, the time available, whether or not issues of life-and-death are involved, and the values of the particular organization. No leader or manager gets it right every time, but training can help to cut down dramatically the number of times that inappropriate choices on the decision-making continuum are made.

LEVELS OF LEADERSHIP

Leadership exists on different levels. There is the team level, where the leader is in charge of 10 to 15 people. The operational leader is responsible for a significant part of the business, such as a business unit, division or key functional department. At the strategic level, the leader, often the CEO, is leading the whole organization. 'Strategic leadership' is actually an expansion of the original, for in Greek, 'strategy' is made up of two words: 'stratos', a large body of people, and the '-egy' ending, which means leadership. Strategy is the art of leading a large body of people.The key to achieving sustainable business success is to have excellence in leadership at all three levels. Strategic, operational and team leaders need to work harmoniously together as the organization's leadership team.

PRINCIPLES OF MOTIVATIONAL LEADERSHIP

A great military general, when speaking to his officers, stated: 'See that your men have reason to respect you.' Respect is earned and can never, and should never, be demanded. We all judge leaders more by what they do than by what they say. In commerce, industry and business, managers who supervise others are, of course, sales-people. They have to sell their ideas and work practices. They have to sell good ideas and good work habits. Successful managers appreciate the power of setting a good example. They realize that they are being watched as they go about their day-to-day tasks and that their own example will carry much greater influence and, of course, produce better results than verbal advice, lecturing or any other communication. Sadly, some managers feel that when they have reached a certain level they are no longer subject to the same standards that they expect from their subordinates. They almost believe that it is their job to tell other people what to do, regardless of whether or not they do it themselves. The great tragedy is that, if they don't believe in something strongly enough to practise it themselves, then telling others to do it does really very little good. We all know that the strengths and weaknesses in any department or organization can often mirror those of the people who run it. If you, as a manager, have difficulty getting the people who work for you to measure up to the standards upon which you insist, how about first taking a look at yourself. Do you measure up to these standards? Are you practising what you preach?

So let's now list the 10 principles of motivational leadership.

1. Set Goals

Set a realistic goal and go for it. People are inspired when they work for a manager with a purpose. As we discussed under 'setting your goals', must be achievable, but as a management style it can be very motivating when managers set higher goals. There is always the risk that you might not achieve them. This doesn't really matter, however, as long as it's not a case of continual failure, as this will cause loss of credibility and will affect people's belief that they can achieve future goals.

2. Set an Example

Recognize that, over a period of time, subordinates tend to become carbon copies of their chief. People do look to their superiors for guidance. You will see in so many different organizations how this emulating, either consciously or sub -consciously, not only filters through to work practices, but also to style of clothes and appearance, the way people communicate with each other, their timekeeping, their convictions and maybe even the newspapers they read. The list is endless.

So once again, what sort of people do you want to have working for you? Or if you are a leader outside the world of business, maybe in the sporting world or in the teaching profession, what sort of results—be they behavioural or communicative—are you hoping for? Remember, it starts with you!

3. Constantly Improve

Be a progressive thinker. Employ the 'how can I do it better?' thought process. Eliminate from your thoughts and your vocabulary 'I am doing my best' and never allow the people who you are leading to think that they are doing their best. As we all know—if we want to face the truth—we can all do better. In being a progressive thinker, one naturally has a thought process that always looks to the future rather than the past. And when undergoing self-analysis ask yourself this question: 'Am I worth more today than I was yesterday or last week, last month or even last year?' For a practising progressive thinker, every day is an opportunity for new experience, to gain new knowledge with the single purpose of being a better person at the end of the day.

4. Give Yourself Time to Think

Spend some time in uninterrupted thought. It's really quite extraordinary and perhaps rather sad that so many leaders just do not allow themselves thinking time, and of those that do, it is not so much allowing themselves as snatching it, often while travelling. As we know, we have been given this incredible asset of a brain with limitless capacity, but at the same time we often inhibit its enormous power.

5. Lead Without Pushing

The most effective leadership is by example and not by edict. The motivated leader will lead, but not necessarily push, show but not necessarily tell.

In most team sports, the captain is normally one of the best players. But one has to accept that the best performer will not necessarily have leadership skills, although this is the norm and a prerequisite for captaincy. There are very few exceptions: Mike Brearley, the ex-English cricket captain, most certainly was one and he is held in very high esteem as being one of the greatest captains of all time. However, he accepted that he was not one of the best cricketers in terms of batting or bowling. Martin Johnson, on the other hand, the ex-England rugby captain, World Cup winner, Lions captain and current England team manager, proves the point. The calibre of that man is, of course, rare, but nevertheless an example for many business leaders to aspire to.

6. Judge by Results

Expect always to be judged by results, as you, the motivated manager and leader, will judge others by results. If you were setting your own standards for a motivational leadership style, would it be one that is results orientated, following the principles that we have already discussed? Or have you created your own judging-by-results culture?

7. Build Confidence

Develop a supreme confidence in yourself and your ability. This supreme confidence will inspire others and this is the motivational leadership style that can be so effective: raising other people's performance to levels they never believed they were capable of. The 'how tos' of building confidence have already been discussed and we know that, when tackling something new, confidence may be low. But just the sheer understanding of this will help to build and retain the confidence—and at the same time will not reduce ability.

8. Expect Criticism

It's regrettable to say, but nonetheless true, that as a person becomes increasingly successful it is only a matter of time before they are criticized. One of the great British characteristics is that we search desperately for a hero, be it from the world of sport, business or politics. However, as soon as we put them onto a pedestal, with a hero's halo above them, the media has to find ways of bringing them back down again. So if you are going to be a good leader, you should be putting your head above the parapet and making yourself vulnerable to criticism, which nearly always emanates from that most harmful and evil of all human feelings–jealousy!

9. Think of the Future

Plan on doing something different tomorrow. If every day you can do something slightly different from what you did yesterday, each time doing a little bit better, you will create an inspirational leadership style that is very motivational. The person who is always looking for something new to do every day has to have a wonderfully progressive mind.

10. Think like a Winner

This is such a good thought process to adopt. When you are confronted with a situation, be it positive or negative, try to imagine how the most successful person that you know would think and then act in the situation. If it is a sporting situation, think of the most successful player in that sport—how would they think and act? If it is a business situation, and let use an example from the sales world, how would the most successful salesperson think and act?

Differences between a Winner and a Loser

1. A winner makes mistakes and says: 'I was wrong.' A loser says: 'It wasn't my fault.'

2. A winner credits his good luck for winning, even though it wasn't luck. A loser credits his bad luck for losing, even though it wasn't luck.

3. A winner works harder than a loser and has more time. A loser is always 'too busy': too busy staying a failure.

4. A winner goes through a problem. A loser goes around it.

5. A winner shows he's sorry by making up for it. A loser says he's sorry but he does the same thing next time.

6. A winner knows what to fight for and what to compromise on. A loser compromises on what he should not and fights for what isn't worth fighting for. Every day is a battle in life, and it is very important that we are fighting for the right things and not wasting time with trivial matters.

7. A winner says: 'I'm good, but not as good as I ought to be.' A loser says: 'Well, I'm not as bad as a lot of people.' A winner looks up to where he is going. A loser looks down at those who've not yet achieved the position he has.

8. A winner respects those who are superior to him and tries to learn from them. A loser resents those who are superior to him and tries to find fault.

9. A winner is responsible for more than his job. A loser says: 'I only work here.'

10. A winner says: 'There ought to be a better way of doing it.' A loser says: 'Why change it? That's the way it's always been done.'

CAUSES OF LEADERSHIP FAILURE

Although it is extremely important to know what to do when leading people, it must be just as important to know what not to do.

1. Inability to organize detail

Whenever a manager admits publicly or to themself that they are too busy to give sufficient attention to any aspect of their work, they are admitting their inability to do their job effectively.

2. Unwillingness to do what they would ask another to do

When occasion demands, and let stress this is only when the occasion demands, the effective manager is always willing to perform the task that he or she would ask another person to do.

It does not matter that the manager may not be able to do it as well as another—if they are unwilling to try, it can be a cause of failure.

3. Expectation of pay for what they know instead of what they do

The world does not pay people for what they know, it pays them for what they do or, perhaps more importantly, what they motivate others to do.

It is all very well having the most brilliant education, passing all the exams and degrees with a brain stacked full of knowledge. But you must remember that this is not what you are paid for. People get paid for what they do rather than what they know.

4. Fear of competition from others

Whatever we fear invariably happens. The manager who fears that one of his followers could take his position is almost sure to realize that fear sooner or later.

So many managers are afraid that their own position is threatened that they try to hold back people below them rather than build them up in order to protect themselves. We have all heard the expression: 'You can't hold good people down.'

5. Lack of creative thinking

Without creative thinking, the manager is incapable of creating plans and setting goals with which to guide staff effectively. It can also be described as lateral thinking.

The blinkered manager will miss opportunities and will not inspire his people.

6. The 'I' syndrome

The manager who claims all the credit for achievements of his or her team is certain to be met with resentment. The completely effective leader will claim none of the credit, but will ensure that, when there is any, it goes to the team.

7. Over-indulgence

In whatever form over-indulgence may manifest itself, not only will it destroy the endurance and the vitality of the manager, but it will also cause a loss of respect from the team. Over-indulgence can be manifested in many and varied forms—from alcohol abuse to womanizing!

8. Disloyalty

The manager who is not loyal to his colleagues, both above him and below him, will not maintain his leadership for very long.

A lack of loyalty is one of the major causes of failure and loss of respect in every walk of life.

> Loyalty is like respect—it is earned and can never be demanded.

9. Emphasis on the 'authority of leadership'

An example of this is: 'Do this or you're fired!' Successful leaders lead by encouraging and not by trying to instil fear in their followers. Instilling fear falls within the category of leadership by force. History has shown that this is an effective form of leadership. It does work—*but it never lasts!*

A manager who uses fear as a tool of motivation will find it effective the first and possibly the second time it is used. But then the power starts to diminish. It is then only a matter of time before authority is destroyed.

10. Emphasis of title

Some managers make a great play of their title and have it displayed on their office door. Usually, the manager who makes too much of his or her title has little else to make very much of.

11. A lack of understanding of the destructive effects of a negative environment

It is utterly impossible to be a great leader or a motivational manager without a deep understanding of the extreme harm caused by a negative environment.

12. A lack of common sense

Perhaps one way of illustrating this list of the 12 major causes of failure in leadership is the manager who becomes so heavenly minded and ultra positive he is no earthly good.

So one must remember, with all human characteristics, the Extremes are dangerous.

MAJOR ATTRIBUTE OF LEADERSHIP

1. A willingness to try the untried

No employee wishes to be led by a manager who lacks courage and self-confidence. It is a positive leadership style that takes on challenging tasks or takes opportunities that have not been tried before.

A successful sales manager will go out and sell when the marketplace is really tough or when the salespeople are under extreme pressure. That manager knows that he or she risks being unsuccessful, but nevertheless, by leading by example, will maintain the motivation of the team.

2. Self-motivation

The manager who cannot motivate himself has not got the slightest chance of being able to motivate others.

3. A keen sense of what is fair

This is a great quality of an effective leader. In order to retain the respect of the team, a manager must be sensitive to what is fair and just. The leadership style whereby all people are treated justly and equally always creates a feeling of security.

4. Definite plans

The motivated leader always has goals and has planned their achievement. He or she plans the work and then works the plan.

5. Decision 'stickability'

The manager who wavers in the decision-making process shows that he is unsure of himself, whereas an effective leader makes a decision after having given sufficient thought to the problem. He even considers the possibility that the decision being taken may turn out to be the wrong one.

Most people who make decisions will get some of them wrong. However, this does not necessarily diminish respect from their followers. Let's be realistic: a manager may make more decisions that are wrong than the followers make that are right, but an effective leader makes the decision and shows his conviction and belief in that decision by sticking to it. The followers then have the strength to fight for that decision as well.

6. The habit of doing more than one is paid for

One of the penalties of leadership is a willingness to do more than is required of one's followers. The manager who arrives before the employees and leaves a little bit later is one example of this attribute of leadership.

7. A positive personality

Followers respect this quality. It not only inspires confidence, but also builds and maintains an enthusiastic team.

8. Empathy

The successful leader must have the ability to put himself in the shoes of his followers—to be able to see the world from their side. He does not have to agree with it but must be able to see how they feel and understand their viewpoint.

9. Mastery of detail

The successful leader understands and carries out every detail of his or her job and, of course, has the knowledge and the skill to master the responsibilities that go with the position.

10. Willingness to assume full responsibility

Another penalty of leadership is the accepted practice of taking responsibility for the mistakes of followers. Should a follower make a mistake, perhaps through incompetence, the leader must consider that it is him- or herself who has failed. If the leader tries to shift this responsibility, he will not remain the leader.

11. Duplication

The successful leader is always looking for ways of duplicating skills in other people. In this way, he develops others and is effectively able to be in many different places at the same time. Perhaps this, of all the necessary attributes, has to be the greatest for leaders– the ability to develop other leaders is vital. One can always judge a leader by the number of people in whom they have duplicated their talents, and those who they have developed and brought into the world as great leaders.

12. A deep belief in their principles

'Unless we stand for smoothing, we will fall for

anything.' Nothing worth achieving is ever very easy. The successful leader has a determination to achieve goals, no matter what obstacles come along, and believes in what he or she is doing with a determination to fight for it.

6

UNDERSTAND THE CAUSES OF DEMOȚIVATION

Just as important as knowing the rules of motivation is to know and be able to recognize the demotivators. The foundation of all motivation, is hope. Without hope, an individual is going to be without motivation. Mankind is a goal-striving animal. The history of mankind goes from one goal achievement to another and it is this looking forward to the future that immeasurably helps towards creating a motivated mind.

A person who lacks motivation or who has been demotivated by others or by circumstances will show through their body language, their appearance and facial expressions how they are feeling. It is essential, therefore, to recognize the outward signs of the unmotivated person. This, of course, is common sense, but owing to the pressure and the pace of life that most people lead, all too often they are not conscious of other people's feelings. This is why it is so important for a motivated manager to be able to experience empathy.

Domestic relationships and arguments in so many cases could be solved by both parties looking at their dispute from the other person's viewpoint. It is so easy to do when one asks oneself: 'Why did he say that?' or 'Why did she say that?' You see, what normally happens is that people react to the words and, of course, to the facial expression, but they don't delve into what *caused* the other person to say those words. Empathy does not mean one has to agree with the other person. Empathy is understanding why the other person says or does what they do. There are those, as we have said, who have no empathy, and then there are those who have too much empathy, which can cause timidity, lack of assertiveness and is expressed by what we would call a lack of confidence. Empathy is no different to the normal distribution curve of life–both extremes limit success.

So what are the outward signs of the unmotivated person?

First, appearance. People can take less care of it when they are not engaged or motivated. This is why it is so important for leaders to be continually appraising colleagues in the endeavour to spot any signs. This can also be widened to the state in which they keep their car and then even to the way they work and the state of their desk or office. Finally, this uncared-for appearance can also be seen in their home.

Their facial expression will have the corners of their mouth turning down instead of up and will convey the body language messages that the brain inside the body may be unhappy, demotivated, unsure or even bitter. Such people are also more likely to experience illness. And then the most important indicator is, of course, what people say. When they start to speak, they instantly give the listener, if they really listen to what is being said, the final indication of the motivated or unmotivated person.

Now let's look at some of the principal causes of demotivation at work.

LACK OF CONFIDENCE

This can often be expressed by the internal feeling of

'Can I do it?' or 'I'm not good enough', 'I'm unqualified, unable...', and so on.

When people lack confidence, it is primarily caused by one of the following three factors:

1. Their confidence has been removed by what somebody else has said–we will look in more detail at this under the third demotivator.

2. It may have been caused by childhood conditioning. Every baby born into the world arrives with a positive brain and during the first few months of its life receives positive input from its parents. As soon as the child starts to move, the positive inputs increase, the 'Yes, you can's, the 'You can do it's. The infant is soon able to stand, the pride of the parents increases and so do the positives.

   Eventually, the first steps are taken. The baby can walk, friends and family are quite naturally invited to share in the pleasure, but as soon as the baby is really able to walk, the inputs can turn dramatically from positive to negative—'Be careful', 'Don't do that', 'Don't touch, you might hurt yourself'... and so that positive brain starts to experience NO–NO conditioning.

3. By past experience conditioning.

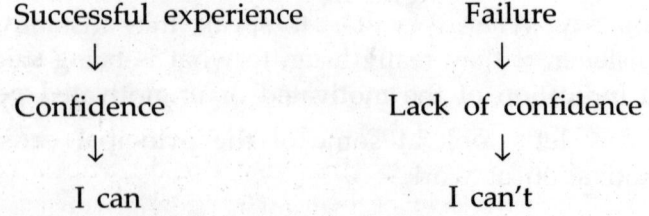

Successful experience	Failure
↓	↓
Confidence	Lack of confidence
↓	↓
I can	I can't

Suppose you are asked to make a speech. Your subconscious will automatically go to recall. If the last speech you gave went down well, the 'Yes I can do it' will come to the forefront. If the last speech was a disaster, then your past experience conditioning will be providing you with the 'I can't' feeling. This, of course, can be overcome, as you will see; but what is important here is to understand how you feel. If you have never given a speech before, then your subconscious recall will be saying 'Can I do it?'

It is therefore essential that, in managing oneself as well as others, you first try to understand the causes that create this lack of confidence. And secondly that you do not become the cause for future lack of confidence. Everybody from time to time if they are doing something new will experience a confidence shake-up. If somebody ever says they never lack confidence it means they are never doing anything new.

An effective manager must therefore not destroy the confidence in others as this will most certainly demotivate. This will also create a loss of trust and loyalty.

UNWANTED WORRIES

The word 'worry' comes from the Anglo Saxon word 'weirgan' which means to strangle, to choke until there is no life left. Worry can almost do that to some people. Worry is, of course, a factor of demotivation. It is the feeling that people have when they are concerned about what will happen if they fail; the fear that if they make a mistake they could lose their job; and perhaps the most obnoxious fear is that of being ridiculed in front of one's colleagues or peers. In some organizations the worry linked to the fear of making a mistake causes the safety and security of no action and certainly no decision making. It is the feeling of 'What happens if I fail?'—it is, in some cases, the fear that I'm going to be criticized in public. It is so important for managers to prevent this culture of worry, as this in turn can lead to people not sleeping well and having a distressing private life.

It is essential for progress and survival for people to make decisions and if decisions are going to be taken, a percentage of them will almost certainly result in mistakes. A motivational management style will never demotivate an individual by punishing that person for a mistake. All the great leaders and entrepreneurs in the world readily admit they make mistakes and errors of judgement. They are just fortunate that the right decisions outweigh the wrong ones.

Leaders will develop a total understanding and a passionate belief that failure is not a person but is an unattractive result. It is of course a change of emphasis— making it clear that, although the results are failing, the people are not failures.

NEGATIVE OPINIONS

This surely has to be the single and most evil demotivator. More success, and potential success, has been destroyed by the negative opinion of people than by any other single factor. Within any organization, if one person becomes negative it spreads almost like a forest fire and everybody becomes negative. Any person who is unable or unwilling to understand fully the danger and effect of negative opinion will never be able to master motivation. It is the harmfulness of what people say to each other: the criticizing, condemning and complaining; the moaning, the griping, the unkind gossip and the negative rumour. Have you noticed that the grapevine in business very rarely produces healthy fruit? It is always diseased. A negative group or team becomes an unproductive group or team. A negative person loses their productive capability. This really is such a destroyer of potential success and achievement that you must understand what is meant by negative talk, comment or communication in any form. Understanding is essential in order for you to be in a position to either prevent or deal with this horrible human characteristic.

First, differentiate between constructive and destructive criticism—welcome the former and ban the latter (make sure, of course, that you practise what you preach). Secondly, create an environment where people will come to you or will attend meetings with ideas about 'How To' rather than 'How Not To'. Thirdly, make sure you have prevented a negative culture by training your people in the effects of negative communication. Fourthly, make sure you and your people are equipped to deal with a negative outbreak if it should occur.

Suppose you have a good idea and you discuss your good idea with a friend and this individual gives you negative feedback. Your idea won't work, it is not the right time, you wouldn't be able to carry it out anyhow... How do you feel? Motivated or demotivated? You know the answer and so do I.

First let ask if you ever seek an opinion or advice from another person, are they the best possible person to give you their opinion? You can ask a taxi driver his opinion of brain surgery and no doubt he will have one, but there must be some question as to the validity of that opinion. *The Experts Speak* by Christopher Cerf and Victor Navasky, published by Pantheon Books.

> Edison said: 'The talking picture will not supplant the regular silent motion picture.'
>
> Aristotle said: 'Women may be said to be an inferior man.'
>
> 'For the majority of people, smoking has a beneficial effect': Dr Ian McDonald, surgeon, quoted in, November.

'The aeroplane will never fly': Lord Haldane.

'Television won't last—it's a flash in the pan': Mary Somerville.

The above were comments from so-called experts. So what chance have any of us got with the bloke we meet in the pub!

Remember if you are on the receiving end of somebody else's negative opinion, it is only an opinion— they may be right or, on the other hand, they may be wrong; and it seems a characteristic of the most successful people in life that they very rarely give a straight negative opinion. They are more likely, when passing on their advice, to look for the worst-case scenario, and then, after checking all the possibilities of success, they end up by giving you more information. With this comes a greater understanding of the subject on which you want an opinion, so that you are better able to form your own opinion and make your own decision.

While on the subject of opinions, new and aspiring politicians should learn how to use the word 'never'– and then never say never.

FEELING OF 'NO FUTURE HERE'

When anyone feels that they have no future they are, of course, going to be demotivated. Some businesses people have to wait for the clichéd 'dead man's shoes'. In other cases, they know there is no chance of promotion as this will go to a member of the ruling family.

In some organizations advancement is determined by the number of years of service, while in other companies all the senior positions are filled from outside.

It must be accepted that it is not necessarily bad practice for businesses not to provide a career path. In many cases people will use their employers as stepping stones to their own objective, which, of course, is perfectly healthy and understandable. What is right is that both the employer and employee should be able to recognize and respect their own terms or position of employment. The 'no future here' feeling can be managed and diminished by good management. If the manager is aware that there may not be career advancements or opportunities within their organization they can at least provide the stimulus and motivation that reduces that no-future-here feeling. They can do this by providing recognition for jobs done well, by changing and sharing responsibilities, by involvement in decision making and, perhaps most importantly, by providing training opportunities.

It is obvious (but nevertheless must be said) that it would be demotivational to provide training for skills that could never be used within that organization.

I FEEL UNIMPORTANT

When a person genuinely feels unimportant they will, of course, be demotivated. This can also be expressed as 'Nobody cares about me', 'I am insignificant', 'I am but a little cog in this large machine'.

This can–like all the demotivators–be so easily prevented by good management. Line managers with leadership and motivational skills know that recognition can remove this feeling. It can be just a 'thank you'; it can be a personal letter from the senior manager of a management team; it can be as simple as the chairman of the company knowing and using the individuals name.

There is a lovely example of a person visiting a building site. On speaking to one bricklayer he asked him what he was doing, to which the bricklayer replied: 'I am laying bricks'. The second bricklayer was asked the same question, to which he replied: 'I am building a wall', and the third bricklayer responded to that same question with: 'I am building a house'.

The third bricklayer obviously felt he was part of the project and he most certainly felt very important.

This is why management style has gone from the 'Big is Beautiful' syndrome to 'Small is Beautiful'. Perhaps the simplest and easiest way of removing this feeling of unimportance is to take active steps instantly to give instead of tan yhem?

'You can get what you want if you help enough other people to get what they want.'

'I DON'T KNOW WHAT'S GOING ON'

This is such a common demotivator when people feel, rightly or wrongly, that they don't know what's going on—nobody bothers to tell them anything, they are always the last to hear.

In an organization where this is a common feeling, information is often communicated via the proverbial grapevine. This information in most cases is frighteningly inaccurate, and is virtually always negative and distorted by gossip. This can all be summed up as poor communication. For many years British managers stopped talking to their workforce and communicated only through the trade unions. What an extraordinary way to manage, motivate and communicate with one's employees! Unions, of course, have a rightful place in a healthy society, but their role is not to communicate between the management and their employees. Again, prevention is so easy. People should be kept informed, they should hear the news from their own bosses and they shouldn't have to know what's going on by reading the national press. They should not have to be dependent on rumour. As we all know, rumour is invariably inaccurate.

DUE TO UNETHICAL REWARDS

Under the laws of motivation we discussed the importance of recognition in the motivation stakes. In any organization where people are promoted, rewarded or recognized for being a member of the right family or due to a personal relationship or even just because 'their face fits', then demotivation will be the effect.

Here is a list of questions exploring the causes of demotivation; fill it in and assess your own organization.

	Yes	No
Is the company policy acceptable?		
Does everyone know the policy?		
Is the policy right for customers?		
Are the core processes suitable for delivery of customer care?		
Is there job security?		
Are relations good with all personnel and management?		
Are work hours impacting on family and home life?		
Do people/you feel valued at work?		

LACK OF TRAINING

The second most common cause of people needing medical treatment for stress is lack of training. With ever-increasing demands for change, people at work are given new responsibilities and new tasks. They are then expected by their managers to carry out tasks according to the managers' expectations, but they are not trained or given guidance. They don't do the job because they don't know how to do it, or they don't do it because of the fear of getting it wrong. They then try to hide the situation and, as a result, feel terribly guilty. Leaders on the other hand will never delegate without fully understanding the consequences, and will also passionately embrace the culture of investing in their people—training and helping them to make sure that those tasks will lead to success.

7

HOW TO MOTIVATE YOURSELF?

Self-motivation is a power that drives us to keep moving ahead. It encourages continuous learning and success, whatever be the scenario. Self-motivation is a primary means of realizing our goals and progressing. It is basically related to our inventiveness in setting dynamic goals for ourselves, and our faith that we possess the required skills and competencies for achieving those challenging goals. We often feel the need for self-motivation.

Following are the ways/techniques for self-motivation:

— *Communicate and talk to get motivated:* Communicating with someone can boost up your energy and make you go on track. Talk with optimistic and motivated individuals. They can be your colleagues, friends, wife, or any one with whom you can share your ideas.

— *Remain optimistic:* When facing hurdles; we always make efforts to find how to overcome them. Also, one should understand the good in bad.

— *Discover your interest area:* If you lack interest in current task, you should not proceed and continue with it. If an individual has no interest in the task, but if it is essential to perform, he should correlate it with a bigger ultimate goal.

— *Self-acknowledgement:* One should know when his motivation level is saturated and he feels like on top of the world. There will be a blueprint that once an individual acknowledge, he can proceed with his job and can grow.

— *Monitor and record your success:* Maintain a success bar for the assignments you are currently working on. When you observe any progress, you will obviously want to foster it.

— *Uplift energy level:* Energy is very essential for self-motivation. Do regular exercises. Have proper sleep. Have tea/coffee during breaks to refresh you.

— *Assist, support and motivate others:* Discuss and share your views and ideas with your friends and peers and assist them in getting motivated. When we observe others performing good, it will keep us motivated too. Invite feedback from others on your achievements.

— *Encourage learning:* Always encourage learning. Read and grasp the logic and jist of the reading. Learning makes an individual more confident in commencing new assignments.

— *Break your bigger goals into smaller goals:* Set a short time deadline for each smaller goal so as to achieve bigger goal on time.

ASSERTIVENESS

Assertiveness is a little like motivation inasmuch as many people feel they should be more assertive or that they are just not assertive enough. Many people seem to want it, but are not quite sure what it really is. Assertion is probably best described as expressing opinions, thoughts and feelings in a non-defensive manner—clearly and openly. It is being able to make requests and to refuse requests that are unacceptable. This sounds simple enough, but in reality many people experience great difficulty in refusing other people's demands as well as in communicating with friends, colleagues or–more often–people at work. Assertion does not mean being heavy-handed, dogmatic, boring or over-bearing. The importance of empathy and of understanding self-confidence. Empathy has to play a major part in being assertive. Assertiveness involves communicating in a way that takes account of other people's feelings. It also has to be an expression of self-confidence.

Fear of Rejection

People who genuinely feel that their style of communication is too submissive and not assertive enough often find that the cause is due to past experience. The cause in many cases is past feelings of rejection–or what the individual may term as rejection. In reality, they are often mistaken. In its most simple definition, rejection is when the person to whom one is communicating replies with or implies the word 'no'. Please do accept that when anybody says 'no' to you it is only ever 'no' at that particular time. It is not 'no' later in the day, tomorrow, next week, next month or next year.

Developing Assertiveness

Many people feel that to develop their assertiveness they need to be more aggressive. The human race reacts very badly to aggression and rejects it, so this feeling cannot be right.

Assertion is an interpersonal skill. It can reflect your habitual way of thinking. It can project your innermost feelings about yourself and, of course, your relationships with others.

Being assertive means that one should communicate clearly, openly and non-defensively. Don't make apologies for yourself unless they are absolutely genuinely due.

Let's look at nine steps that help the individual to develop their assertiveness.

1. Expect to be anxious

It is quite normal and totally acceptable in the field of human communication that everybody, from time to time, feels anxious when they say what they think or feel, and if any individual honestly says they never feel anxious, they must have no understanding, empathy or feelings about anybody else.

So don't be embarrassed. Your anxious feeling is totally acceptable–it is because you care.

2. Build your confidence

Suffice to say here that confidence can be like a habit– bad habits take time to develop and are created by continual practice and repetition until at some stage they become hard to lose. But they do take time to develop fully.

Good habits are exactly the same. They take time to form and must be continually practised. Good habits, when they come to fruition, are just as difficult to get out of.

3. Believe in yourself

If you do not already fully believe in yourself, then start NOW! Because if you don't believe in yourself, you are making it very hard for anybody else to do so.

If you think you are beaten, you are
If you think you are not, you aren't

If you'd like to win but think you can't
It's almost certain you won't
Life's battles don't always go
To the stronger or faster person
But sooner or later the person who wins
Is the person who thinks they can

4. Watch and listen to what others communicate to you

'Watch' means be aware of body language. The signals that are conveyed by a person's body language can provide a great deal of information. There are approximately 750,000 body language signals, some of which are very difficult to control.

These signals will invariably give you more accurate information than what somebody actually says.

Being assertive does not mean just getting your viewpoint across. It is a combination of being able to listen and persuade. As all sales people know, these are essential ingredients when selling your ideas.

Perhaps one of the keys to being more assertive is to understand, then know through belief, how easy it is to sell one's ideas.

In developing this stage of your assertiveness self-training, practise listening to another person's viewpoint without submissively surrendering your own.

Let remind you again: ask yourself 'Why did he say that?' or 'Why did she say that?'

5. Consider the situation

This means that, in order to communicate effectively and assertively, give yourself time to think and consider the situation that needs to be handled. It will strengthen your confidence and your ability to communicate your message.

There is that lovely expression: 'Act in haste, repent at leisure.'

Everybody has a right to consider before responding, and in helping yourself to develop the right thought process, try thinking what the end result is you want to achieve. In so much poor communication, people try to score points or to win an argument. In the sales world, the saying is: 'You can win the argument, but you lose the sale.' So why score points? Decide the result that you want and this will help you to think about a positive solution. Good thinking means the brain should be allowed to be flexible. Don't allow your thinking process to become entrenched, as it will be difficult to think in any other way.

6. Plan your response

When thinking about a situation that needs resolving, be sure to check that the problem you are solving is the important issue and not just a smokescreen hiding the real crux of the matter.

So, in planning your response, decide when and how you will make it. In your mental preparation, come to terms with yourself and accept the fact that in some instances others involved could get upset or angry. A truly positive thinking person always plans for the best, clearly has in their mind a positive result, but has also looked at the worst possible result and has a contingency plan just in case. Having mentally prepared for the worst possible result, it is then deleted from the thought process of the positive thinker's mind.

7. Make your point

If, for some extraordinary reason, you get very nervous or you feel very anxious, take a couple of deep breaths. This normally settles the nervous system, generating oxygen in the blood-stream.

Be open and non-defensive. Do not imagine that the other person is tuned in to your level of thinking. Do not rely upon their imagination and don't communicate with the feeling 'Well, I hope they get the message'. There must be no misunderstanding and, of course, no sarcasm. In getting your point of view across effectively, please accept that, to a certain extent, person-to-person communication is a sales process. Its aim is to persuade somebody to see clearly the result of what you wish to achieve.

The steps necessary to achieve this result are never as important as communicating a clear picture of what the result could be like.

8. No nicely

This is probably the most important characteristic of an assertive person—being able to say no nicely. It appears that a lack of assertiveness is more common in women than it is in men.

9. Be positive

Finally, Always be Positive—happy, cheerful and smiling.

People who communicate with a cheerful and positive expression somehow always seem to get their message across.

Say something nice, not creepy—a general compliment, for example. Be willing to give praise and do so enthusiastically. People will feel safer with you when they know how you really feel—remember, if we don't stand for something, we'll fall for anything.

SELF-MOTIVATION BY BUILDING SELF-CONFIDENCE

The most valuable asset for most people is also the least

valued. It is an asset that, with the right care, can appreciate dramatically. It is an asset that is taken for granted and that is impossible to put a price on. This asset, of course, is one's brain and the thinking processes that accompany it. Researchers continually tell us that only a small proportion of the human brain is still understood and used. The greatest development as we proceed through the 21st century will be a greater understanding and fuller usage of the brain.

So why is this relevant to self-motivation? Because, very simply, there has to be a direct corollary between self-belief and personal motivation.

If you can accept that your most valuable asset is your brain, it is then worthwhile accepting some basic principles on its function. For example, whatever you put in, you will get back out. The brain operates in a similar fashion to the modern computer. The brain, moreover, has the powers of reason and creativity that the computer does not. So, if you accept that the brain is the most incredible storage area, it then becomes essential to take care in what you are asking it to store. Some people will have a brain filled full of negative thoughts and experiences.

So when confronted with a new opportunity or challenge, their brains, on being asked a question, will deliver a negative answer.

1. Get Rid of Excuses

So many people hold themselves back by making unjustifiable and largely untrue excuses to themselves, such as:

— 'I can't.'

— 'I am unable to because...'

— 'I haven't had the right education.'

— 'I am not assertive enough.'

— 'I am too old.'

— 'I am too young.'

— 'I suffer from poor health.'

— 'I am not lucky.'

— 'I'm never in the right place at the right time.'

— 'I didn't go to the right schools.'

— 'It's my family background.'

— 'I was born under the wrong birth sign.'

Excuses. You can find an excuse for almost anything, so in building confidence, never make an excuse.

2. Use Picture Power

First, let ask you two questions. How do you feel about yourself? What is your own self-image? You will be able to answer by saying that you are proud of yourself, you feel good about yourself–but you would like to be better.

We have all heard the expression 'Seeing is believing.' The brain, with its limitless capacities, can help you immeasurably to achieve life's ambitions if you give it the chance. Picture yourself as the person you want to be. Clearly visualize whatever it is you want to achieve. The more you think about it, the greater the certainty will be of a positive result.

There is another expression that says: 'What we think about, we become', although this can work in a negative way as well as a positive one.

If you continually allow your thoughts to dwell on illnesses and bad health, you almost certainly will experience the ailments that you think about. If you continually think about negative results in your relationship or business career, they will come to fruition. So in building confidence by using the brain's picture-power image process, it is essential to make sure that what you are thinking and vividly seeing is positive. It must be conducive to your own self-image and its improvement, and your thoughts must be towards your goals, aspirations and happiness in life.

Think about what you want, not what you don't want. Go to sleep thinking positive ideas. Create positive images of successful experiences, and endeavour to make this a habit. This 'picture power' involves visualizing; your brain is used to doing this, as it regularly visualizes future happenings. The great sports people of the world concentrate on the result before an event, attempting to remove all distractions from the mind. You should do a similar thing; from today, get into the habit of visualizing the positive and expect the best.

3. Don't Fear Failure

Fear of failure reduces confidence and quite naturally self-motivation too.

When facing a new opportunity or challenge, ask yourself what is the worst that can happen, and what might be termed as failure. Let remind you again, failure is not a person, only an unsavoury result.

The danger with a lot of positive thinking training is that some people can become unbearably and unrealistically positive–so heavenly minded that they are no earthly good.

A good balance is essential. One must be realistic: having looked at the worst-case scenario and thought about how to handle a situation should it arise–in other words, having planned a contingency–remove that thought completely and concentrate on your plan for success.

But whatever you do, don't fear failure. This holds so many people back from ever trying, doing or achieving because they are unable to come to terms with the possibility that they might fail.

Some people actually never try anything because this fear of failure has been cultivated in their brain for years. They think about it daily so they never actually do anything and in turn become unconfident, unsure and unhappy. Let remind you of that wonderful quote: 'The only way to conquer fear is to keep doing the thing you fear to do.'

Before leaving the subject of failure, there are some people who are motivated by the fear of failure. While they are motived by the fear, they never visualize themselves actually failing, and that is the crucial difference.

4. Consider Your Appearance

Have you ever been to an evening engagement where everybody apart from yourself was dressed in dinner jacket or evening dress? If it were to happen, you might experience a confidence crisis. It would be the same brain, the same body, but your outward appearance would have let you down. You must understand the importance of outer appearance and spend money to make sure it is looking good, so that the inside has a chance to become good. But, like everything else, be realistic. Some people overindulge in their appearance and end up only feeding their own ego.

5. Keep a Record of Past Successes

Everybody has successes in their lives. Equally, everybody has down spells when they either lose confidence or experience a reversal of their pattern of success. When this happens, it should be the responsibility of the individual to bounce back again. A good idea is to compile a record of past success. Think back to your earliest memory of success. It may be at your first school, winning the egg and spoon race. It may be the congratulations received on a drawing or painting. But from that earliest memory, recall every success experience you have had in your life.

Whatever method used, add to it every bit of success that comes your way. Then, when later faced with a possible loss of confidence, you can turn to that record and refresh your most valuable asset with the memory of some of those success experiences. This will diminish the feeling of self-doubt or loss of confidence that circumstances have provoked.

Motivation can only perpetuate on the back of hope. To motivate oneself, one has to have hope. Hope, of course, is looking forward to the future. Therefore, for individuals to motivate themselves, they must be responsible for creating their own hope. Truly self-motivated individuals do not allow their hope to be out of their control or provided by others–by the government, by the world political scene, by the weather or any other factor that is not in their direct control.

MOTIVATE YOURSELF BY SETTING GOALS

The extraordinary thing about goals is that so few people actually do decide what they want. You've no doubt heard the expression: 'A person who is going nowhere normally gets there.' But it seems quite extraordinary when you ask people what they want, how few really do *know* what they want. People talk in glib terms of 'I want to be successful' or 'I'd like to be a millionaire' or 'I want happiness'. But they actually don't know what they really want and then are unhappy and negative because they haven't got it.

What the mind can accurately conceive and believe, it is forced to achieve. The history of mankind has been a history of goal achievement. Leading psychologists now regard the brain and the nervous system as highly complex automatic goal-seeking mechanisms. So we all have the equipment necessary to achieve what we really want if we care to use it. And if you want something badly enough and you have the equipment that will help you to get it, make use of it!

So here are the stages of goal setting and of achievement.

1. List Your Desires

Make a list of all the things you really want, both long-term and short-sterm, in your business life and in your private life, both tangible and intangible.

In making this list, be realistic. Many motivational speakers say to their audiences: 'Set big goals.' They are wrong. And it can be dangerous. It may sound highly motivational in a convention hall, but the danger is that short-term goals that are too big don't become believable and are not achieved. The goal setter then becomes demotivated and, in some cases, never tries again. Big goals can be set long-term. They should be staged and there is nothing wrong whatsoever in enlarging the size of one's thinking to become a 'big thinking' person. Let remind you once again: we become what we think about.

Don't put down certain items on your goal sheet because you think you ought to. The only thoughts you put down should be the ones that you really, really, really want.

Don't just put down monetary goals. They must be turned into something tangible unless they are the removal of a debt. Money is required to be spent on something specific that you want and should not be an end in itself. Making your list can be a lot of fun but it's a serious business. Compiling this list is something that should be completely private unless you have a very close relationship with another person, in which case one's goals should be shared and discussed. Many marriages or relationships break-up because the two people involved have different goals. It is quite extraordinarily how few people do spend any time in thinking about what they really want to do, achieve or experience in their life.

2. Select a Goal

Now select from your list of goals a primary one, taking into account these three points that are so important to remember:

(a) It should be high enough to be worth the effort.

(b) It should be achievable in months, not years, and ideally within a maximum of three months.

It must be something you can reach quite quickly. As we all know, success breeds success. It will build your confidence and will prove that the system works for you. But above everything else, the human brain is more responsive to the immediate short-term than the longer-term.

(c) Be realistic about any financial considerations if money is involved.

3. Define Your Target

Define your chosen goal in complete detail. At this stage of goal setting, it is important for your most valuable asset to be your focus, and to be crystal clear as to what the goal is. Your goal might be that you'd like to lose weight, but losing weight is not a goal. Be specific—how much weight exactly do you want to lose? The goal may be: 'I would like to be fitter.' Exactly what does fitness mean for that individual? It may mean being able to do 20 press-ups and run two miles. Your target, therefore, must be totally quantifiable and measurable. Another goal might be: 'I would like to be promoted.' Promoted to what? What position, what title, what responsibility, etc? For somebody else, it may be that they would like a new car. Is the car to be new or second hand? Which make and model, what colour and which extras? Let remind you of the saying: 'What the mind of man can accurately conceive and believe, it is forced to achieve.'

4. Use Your Subconscious

Imagine that you have achieved your goal. Again, we are talking about using your most valuable asset. Let your conscious and subconscious mind vividly imagine you being in the position of attaining your goal.

Your brain can become your greatest ally and supporter. It can be your greatest fan if you give it a chance. It will most certainly be your most productive employee if you give it the right training. Continuing this analogy, some people think their brain is their most expensive employee, as it always thinks the worst, makes all the excuses and continually sees the negative rather than the positive.

5. Set a Deadline

Now set a deadline for your goal's achievement. Decide the exact date by which you want that goal. We all respond to deadlines. If we know a plane is leaving at a certain time, we make an effort to catch it. So you must decide when you want to achieve your goal.

Isn't it funny how, every year, people say that they will do their Dipawali shopping earlier, or even do it during the year? But every year,Dipawali shopping seems to be done by the vast majority in the last two weeks. The human brain does respond to deadlines!

6. Carry a Reminder

Carry your goals. Every person who is ambitious and striving for achievement should carry their goals with them as a reminder and a purpose.

If you ever find that you are distracted or you experience a setback or perhaps—even more commonly—somebody else tries to deflect you from your goals, you may find it useful to have a copy of your goals on your person—either written in a diary or on a card—to act as a constant reminder. This helps you to remember your purpose.

Your Personal Plan

This now leads to the final part of goal setting and achievement. What we have done so far is build the stages of deciding what you really want and training the brain to become your most effective and profitable employee. The final stage is to prepare a plan.

Of course, this is a farcical situation, as in the real world the owners of the liner, having decided the destination and the date of departure, etc, would have prepared a master plan for the conduct of that voyage. The route would have been decided, as well as stopping-off points, the number of crew, the tonnage of fuel and food, the number of tickets that needed to be sold and the agencies that would have been employed to sell them. Every single detail would have been planned well in advance. The same must be done for your life and your goals. The liner, without its master plan, would almost certainly have become shipwrecked on some rocks. So in preparing the plan for your own goals, the simple stages are these: Take a sheet of paper, write the exact goal at the top with the date of its required achievement and then make a list of all the stages necessary.

Having completed the plan, now all you have to do is concentrate on the first stage and, when that is completed, go on to the next stage. Each stage of the plan should have its own dated deadline. What we have done is to break that goal down into a series of small easily manageable and even more believable simple steps, using one of those great principles from the eight laws of success that says:

Success by the inch is a Cinch and by the Yard it's Hard

Goal: To lose 14 lb Start date: Goal date:

Action plan	Action date
Have complete doctor's health check	_____
Select suitable diet	_____
Purchase diet plan provisions	_____
Start exercise plan:	
Week 1 Lose 2 lb	_____
Week 2 Lose 2 lb (4 lb)	_____
Week 3 Lose 2 lb (6 lb)	_____
Week 4 Lose 2 lb (8 lb)	_____
Week 5 Lose 2 lb (10 lb)	_____
Week 6 Lose 2 lb (12 lb)	_____
Week 7 Lose 2 lb (14 lb)	_____

The above is a simple plan. Concentrate on one stage at a time and tick off each stage when it is achieved.

This is the formula for goal achievement. It is infallible and relies on simple common sense, so why doesn't everybody get what they want in life? There are three very simple reasons:

1. They don't believe they can because of life's negative conditioning.

2. They haven't been shown how.

3. They don't really want to, and therefore aren't prepared to pay the price of a little bit of work or effort in order to achieve their goals.

Let's now move on to a few more ideas that help towards the building of self-motivation.

Right Place, Right Time

Some people convince themselves that they are just not lucky. However, it must be remembered that there is a great difference between luck and chance. Chance is the lottery win or the horse that comes in first. Luck is something that the majority of us can control.

So many successful people often say 'Well, I've been lucky' or 'I've had a stroke of luck', but this invariably comes down to being in the right place at the right time. In order to be in the right place at the right time that individual has most certainly done something to be there. They were not just sitting at home hoping to become lucky.

Luck is best broken down into the mnemonic:

— Labour
— Under
— Correct
— Knowledge

Labour is doing something. The correct knowledge is knowing where you are today, knowing where you want to be and having a plan to get there. We have just covered this in goal setting and achievement.

Right Company

In keeping yourself motivated you must be aware of the

company you keep. Are the people that you meet or surround yourself with positive or negative? If you are continually mixing with negative people who are criticizing, condemning and complaining, finding fault with everything and everybody, it is almost certain that, however positive you are, you will start to conform. The reverse is also true. If you meet and circulate amongst people who are positive, enthusiastic, who have goals, they will, of course, have hope. They are most likely to be motivated. Therefore, you must continually check who you are meeting and talking with, and, in keeping your own motivational level high, avoid to the best of your ability people who are negative. Let's be realistic, it may be a close member of your family or a loved one who is negative. Ask yourself 'Why did she say that?' or 'Why did he say that?' It is the empathy–ego balance that we have already discussed. But avoid negative people wherever you can.

Self-management

Self-management does play an active part in the make-up of the self-motivated person–doing the important and often unpleasant tasks before the pleasurable ones. People sometimes described as having a weaker character than others will often have difficulty with their own self-management, and will do the jobs that please them or neglect to do the tasks that are important.

Don't Retire

Don't retire, just at some stage stop working for a living. It is completely unnecessary to put one's brain into retirement mode, as this is not conducive to self-motivation. But on a business note, there is far too much wastage of talent, particularly in the so-called professions of accountancy and the law. Firms are set up with partners and equity partners. At a given age these people have to retire. In the vast majority of cases, this does not demonstrate a customer care culture to the clients. Relationships that have developed over many years are suddenly broken up, and the customer's contact in the firm has gone.

The firm suffers because it loses an immense amount of experience. Equity partners should release their equity so that others in the firm can benefit—the firm can bring in new talent, but the partners should cut down their time at work. Maybe after a given age, they should do four days a week, then three days, two days and one day until such time as is decided. It is very difficult for the majority of people suddenly to switch from a lifetime's work to no work at all. There are of course exceptions where people have so many hobbies and interests and also sufficient income to give them great joy and fulfilment in the period of their life when they stop working for a living. The word 'retire' is a frightening word. Countless thousands of people dedicate themselves to their employment and their company and then look forward to their retirement. Statistics show the horrifying results of how many die within one or two years of their retirement.

The retirement that they were looking forward to was a goal, and having achieved that goal there then came the vacuum with nothing to look forward to doing or achieving. They had not prepared or planned those wonderful years when they did not have to work for a living. Nobody should ever retire, they should just stop working for a living.

Motivate Yourself by Motivating Others

Finally, in building and maintaining one's own self-motivation, one of the greatest and finest techniques (which may sound glib, but nevertheless is emphatically true and effective) is to motivate somebody else.

As always, let's touch on the principle first that says:

Whatever you Hand out in life, you get back.

This law—again from the laws of success—goes on to say that there is a tenfold return.

So to motivate another person can be as simple as a smile. It is quite uncanny that while walking down a street, or even sitting in a traffic jam in your car, how a big smile offered to somebody else is returned with a smile. And isn't it hard not to be motivated when you are smiling? One of the great distinctions between humankind and the animal world is the ability to laugh.

Almost every problem in the world can be resolved with a sense of humour. We remove the pressures and the worry with a laugh and a joke.

8

HOW TO MOTIVATE
YOUR EMPLOYEES?

Employees are the building blocks of an organization. Organizational success depends on the collective efforts of the employees. The employees will collectively contribute to organizational growth when they are motivated.

"I am in this job because I have no other option." If this is what an employee of your company feels, read on to know how this statement can be changed to something more positive—"I love what I do."First things first— whose responsibility is it to ensure that an employee loves his job? While an employee would say—the employer, the human resource experts have a different point of view which sounds fair. It's both the employer and the employee who should work together to make work fun for each other.It is interesting to know here, that employees do not rank 'salary' as the top factor in determining whether they like their jobs or not. What is important to them then—the opportunity to do what is 'important'.

Almost all the employees would like to feel part of the big picture and would want to contribute to the organizational goals in some way or the other. Doing the mundane, routine work will never excite them-what excites them is-work that challenges them to use their talent. While salary and promotions could do a great job of demotivating people if handled ineffectively, they aren't so much effective in motivating people.

So then what needs to be done for effective motivation at workplace?

— *Link Rewards directly to Performance*: An organization should adopt a fair reward structure which provides incentive to the most deserving employee. Have an incentive structure in place doesn't solve the problem... what makes it workable is the employees trust in the system and believe that they will be rewarded if they perform well.

— *Compliment employees*: Even though an employee's name has not appeared in the list of people getting incentives, go ahead and compliment that employee for a job well done—no matter how small. There is nothing more satisfying to an employee than a pat on his back.

— *Be transparent:* While there may be some strategic decisions which you might want to share with the employees at a later stage, make sure employees do not give in to the rumours. Stay in touch with the employees.

— *Work on your PDP*: Every employee is responsible for his/her own career. He/she should work towards his 'Personal Development Plan' [PDP] as discussed and agreed by his manager. Find out what are the training company offers and which is best suited to his development needs. How this will motivate you—remember training always enhance your career.

— *Participate and Network Employees:* Remember you work for a company where a one-on-one attention might not be possible. Do not wait for an invitation to participate in a discussion. If you are a part of a forum, then you have full right to express your opinion and be a part of the process. Expressing yourself is a good way of motivating yourself

THEORY OF MOTIVATING EMPLOYEES

Most of us at some stage in lives are confronted with another person, who could be an employee, friend or family member, of whom we find ourselves thinking 'If only I could motivate them. There must be something that would give them some get up and go' or 'What on earth can I do to change their attitude and get them turned on to life?' Many managers are continually confronted with this situation–how to motivate individuals in their employ. You should always ask yourself the question, 'Why do you want to motivate that individual?' If it's a member of your family or a close friend it is normally because that person is not fulfilling their real potential. They are missing out on opportunities and are not happy or contented with themselves.

With an employee, to a certain extent, the same applies. You may believe a person has greater potential than they are exhibiting and, as an employer, it is your responsibility to maximize their potential and performance and, of course, the results of other employees. Is the lack of motivation being caused by one of the demotivators already suggested, or is there another root cause? Ask yourself–why is he or she demotivated? And be prepared to accept the answer and possibly the blame for being the cause. If you are the cause, it is your responsibility to act–and possibly change.

It is impossible to motivate if inhibiting conditions are not conducive to motivating the person. The tragedy is that most managers won't conduct a self-inquisition because they fear the reply and won't accept that they are the cause. Now suppose that if, after your own total self-inquisition, the lack of motivation is not caused by the environment, your management style or some of the other demotivating factors in your control, you can now move to the two fundamental stages in the theory of motivating the person:

— Stage 1: Find out what they really want.

— Stage 2: Show them how to get it.

What Do they Want?

So how do you find out what somebody really wants? The simple answer is, of course, to ask them. But let's be realistic, if you were to walk up to one of your employees and ask them in front of their workmates what they really want, one thing is sure: you are not going to get a true answer.

This should only be done in complete privacy and can normally only be approached over a period of time when the employee has developed trust in their employer or manager.

Alternatively, you can find out through observation and, of course, by listening to conversations during relaxation periods. You must accept, as we have already discussed, that a lot of people really don't know what they want and they are unhappy because they haven't got it. This leads to an inner frustration that is not conducive to being a motivated individual. Now if somebody doesn't know what they want, it is extremely difficult to motivate them. Many young people leaving school, college or university are unsure as to what career or job they really want to get into. Many of these young people suffer enormous frustration, and in some cases a tremendous loss of self-confidence when they see their colleagues progressing and striving on in their own chosen careers.

There is no simple solution when helping somebody to find out what they really want. The common sense approach says that the caring leader or manager will help to broaden the thinking of the individual by conversation—by talking and suggesting—but this must in no way be demanding. You must not impose your own aspirations or goals, as this becomes manipulation. In some business environments, a person's goals can be discovered by exposure to other work situations in different departments. Sometimes it may be necessary to send the person on out-placement. However, many individuals do solve this problem themselves eventually.

How can they get it?

The second stage—showing the person how to get what they really want—sounds easier than it is in reality. But once you know what it is a person really wants to do, achieve or own, you can in most cases plan a strategy to help that person achieve their own goals. This is where the really effective manager comes into his or her own. Sometimes the first stage may be to give the person an opportunity to be involved in some further training. Good training is highly motivating for those who are fortunate enough to receive it. In Britain, we undervalue the importance of giving people exposure to further knowledge and skill development.

Research has shown that investing in people and giving them chances to enhance their skills are more conducive towards staff retention. It used to be believed that, by training people, companies would lose them to the competition—the opposite is in fact the case.

In other cases, it may be as simple as working out a career path. With a hobby or in the sporting world, a similar strategy is often adopted, planning a strategy for development.

Employers must accept that if they do not have the vehicle of opportunity to satisfy the goal or the ambition of the individual, that person will move on to new pastures and new career opportunities. Long gone are the days when people joined a company and stayed there for the remainder of their working lives. In some instances, headhunters, recruiters and personnel officers will actually turn people down if they have been with one company for too long a period. It is far better to have an open style of management whereby it is accepted by the manager and the employee that at some stage the employee will be moving on. It is far healthier when the employer takes pride and personal satisfaction from seeing their ex-employees advancing successfully through their careers and achieving outstanding results.

IDEAS FOR MOTIVATING EMPLOYEES

Below mentioned are some tips for motivating the staff/employees in an organization:

Be a good listener

To have any chance at all of inspiring the person, one has to have the confidence and the respect of the individual. This must mean, therefore, that the motivator has to become, to a certain extent, a confidant. We have all heard the expression: 'A problem shared is a problem halved; a joy that is shared is a joy that is doubled.' Therefore, employees, associates and colleagues should have the knowledge that you are approach -able, that they can speak to you, that they won't get bawled at, that you will always give them a fair hearing and that you will be prepared to listen to their problems and worries.

Be trustworthy

It follows on that if you are going to be a confidant and have the respect of others, you do not pass on what is told to you. When somebody tells you their secret, they should be totally secure and confident that it will remain as it should be–a secret. So many managers do not retain the loyalty or respect of their subordinates because they are unable to keep their mouths shut. It is no wonder that the people who are good listeners as well as having the integrity not to pass on confidences invested in them by others will always attract people into their company.

Catch them doing something right

There are many varied ways of raising a person's motivational level and perhaps one of the simplest of all involves utilizing that great expression: 'Catch them doing something right.' All managers will tell staff when they do something wrong, but very few managers tell their people when they do it right.

Criticism sounds best when the result is criticized, not the person.

Show you believe in them

People will rise to the level of belief that their manager has in them. So, in order to inspire an individual to greater levels of achievement or performance, you, 'the inspirator', must believe they can do it and demonstrate your belief in them with expressions like 'I know you can do it', 'You're very good at this' or 'This is one of your strong points.' You must not only show your belief and, of course, confidence in the individual concerned, but let this be seen and heard by their peers. Of course, you must be realistic, and not diminish your own credibility by using a 'You're good at that'-type phrase about something the individual is manifestly incompetent at. If these guidelines are followed, people will often rise to the level of achievement according to the belief that you have in them.

Be a good news carrier

The motivator has to motivate, so always have something encouraging to say. Make sure you are the sort of person who you would like to meet and take inspiration from.

Set challenges

Some people have a short fuse; others have a long fuse. Some get started on the success ladder whilst still at school and others are still on the first rung at the age of 50. Rupert Murdoch, the press and media baron, now in his late seventies, has often been described as the most powerful man in the world and continually looks to acquire new media opportunities.

Be careful with the negative challenge

This is almost the same as point 6 above, but is said with ill humour, little goodwill and a lack of belief. The even more dangerous extension is the negative challenge that can become an insult. A management style occasionally used involves a manager ignoring an individual in their team if they are consistently under-performing. Let emphasise once again that this is an extremely dangerous form of motivation and, if successful, does not build up the management/employee relationship. But, if having achieved success through this form of motivation, time will build a bond if the manager is truly a motivator.

Avoid sarcasm

Sarcasm is very rarely understood and is usually misinterpreted. It is certainly not a motivational style of communication if the motivator wants the other person to listen and respond to what they say. Sarcastic communicators think they are funny. They are, of course, very unfunny and sooner or later it makes people cynical. Cynicism and sarcasm can never lead to a motivational form of communication.

Attract people who achieve successes

On fine warm days, the worker bees go out to gather the pollen, fill their honey sacks and return to the hive. Are you the sort of person who other people want to return to when they have achieved some success? Let also ask, who do you want to tell when you have achieved some success? Who do you want to share that joy or pleasure with? To motivate another person, you must be the sort of person who they instantly want to tell over the telephone or by calling to see you, and your response should always be one of genuine enthusiasm, pleasure, interest and genuinely complimentary. You attract more bees with honey than you do with vinegar.

Evaluate yourself

In order to motivate, encourage and control your staff's behaviour, it is essential to understand, encourage and control your own behaviour as a manager. Work upon utilizing your strengths and opportunities to neutralize and lower the negative impact of your weaknesses and organizational threats. The manager should adopt the approach "You're OK - I'm OK".

Be familiar with your staff

The manager should be well acquainted with his staff.

The more and the better he knows his staff, the simpler it is to get them involved in the job as well as in achieving the team and organizational goals. This will also invite staff's commitment and loyalty. A cordial superior-subordinate relationship is a key factor in job-satisfaction.

Provide the employees certain benefits

Give your staff some financial and other benefits. Give them bonuses, pay them for overtime, and give them health and family insurance benefits. Make sure they get breaks from work. Let them enjoy vacations and holidays.

Participate in new employees induction programme

Induction proceeds with recruitment advertising. At this point of time, the potential entrants start creating their own impressions and desires about the job and the organization. The manner in which the selection is conducted and the consequent recruitment process will either build or damage the impression about the job and organization. Thus, the manager must have a say in framing the advertisement and also in the selection and recruitment process. After the decision about the candidate is made, the manager must take personal interest in the selected joinee's joining date, the family relocation issues, cost of removal, etc. Being observed by the new recruit and your entire team / staff to be involved completely, will ensure a persuasive entry in the organization.

Provide feedback to the staff constantly

The staff members are keen to know how they are performing. Try giving a regular and constructive feedback to your staff. This will be more acceptable by the staff. Do not base the feedback on assumptions, but on facts and personal observations. Do not indulge in favouritism or comparing the employee with some one else. Sit with your staff on daily or weekly basis and make sure that feedback happens. This will help in boosting employee's morale and will thus motivate the staff.

Acknowledge your staff on their achievements

A pat on the back, some words of praise, and giving a note of credit to the employee/staff member at personal level with some form of broad publicity can motivate the staff a lot. Make it a point to mention the staff's outstanding achievements in official newsletters or organization's journal. Not only acknowledge the employee with highest contribution, but also acknowledge the employee who meets and over exceeds the targets.

Ensure effective time management

Having control over time ensures that things are done in right manner. Motivate your staff to have "closed" times, i.e., few hours when there are no interruptions for the staff in performing their job role so that they can concentrate on the job, and "open" times when the staff freely communicate and interact. Plan one to one sessions of interaction with your staff where they can ask their queries and also can get your attention and, thereby, they will not feel neglected. This all will work in long run to motivate the staff.

Have stress management techniques in your organization

Create an environment in which you and your staff can work within optimum pressure levels. Ensure an optimistic attitude towards stress in the workplace. Have training sessions on stress management, and ensure a follow-up with group meetings on the manner stress can be lowered at work. Give your staff autonomy in work. Identify the stress symptoms in employees and try to deal with them.

Use counselling technique

The employees'/staff feelings towards the work, their peer, their superiors and towards the future can be effectively dealt through the staff counseling. Counselling provides an environment, incentive and support which enable the employee to achieve his identity.

Give the employees learning opportunities

Employees should consistently learn new skills on the job. It has been well said by someone that with people hopping jobs more often than required and organizations no longer giving job security to employees, the young blood employees specifically realize that continuing learning is the best way to remain employable. Opportunities should be given to the employees to develop their skills and competencies and to make best use of their skills. Link the staff goals with the organizational goals.

Set an example for your staff/subordinates

Be a role model for your staff. The staff would learn from what you do and not from what you say/claim. The way you interact with your clients/customers and how do you react later after the interaction is over have an impact upon the staff. The staff more closely observes your non-verbal communication (gestures, body language). Being unpunctual, wasting the organization's capital, mismanaging organization's physical equipments, asking the staff to do your personal work, etc. all have a negative impact on the staff. Try setting an example for your staff to follow.

Smile often

Smiling can have a tremendous effect on boosting the morale of the staff. A smiling superior creates an optimistic and motivating work environment. Smiling is an essential component of the body language of confidence, acceptance and boldness. Smile consistently, naturally and often, to demonstrate that you feel good and positive about the staff who works for you. It encourages new ideas and feedback from the staff. The staff does not feel hesitant and threatened to discuss their views this way.

Ensure effective communication

In order to motivate your staff, indulge in effective communication such as avoid using anger expressions, utilize questioning techniques to know staff's mindset and analysis rather than ordering the staff what to do, base your judgements on facts and not on assumptions, use relaxed and steady tone of voice, listen effectively and be positive and helpful in your responses. Share your views with the staff.

Develop and encourage creativity

The staff should be encouraged to develop the creativity skills so as to solve organizational problems. Give them time and resources for developing creativity. Let them hold constant brainstorming sessions. Invite ideas and suggestions from the staff. They may turn out to be very productive.

Don't be rigid. Be flexible

Introduce flexibility in work. Allow for flexible working hours if possible. Let the employees work at home occasionally if need arises. Do not be rigid in accepting ideas from your staff. Stimulate flexible attitudes in the employees who are accountable to you by asking what changes they would like to bring about if given a chance.

Adopt job enrichment

Job enrichment implies giving room for a better quality of working life. It means facilitating people to achieve self-development, fame and success through a more challenging and interesting job which provides more promotional and advancement opportunities. Give employees more freedom in job, involve them in decision-making process, show them loyalty and celebrate their achievements.

Respect your team

Respect not only the employees' rights to share and express their views, and to be themselves, but their time too. This will ensure that the employees respect you and your time. Make the staff feel that they are respected not just as employees/workers but as individuals too.

9

HOW TO MOTIVATE A TEAM?

The difference between a team and a group is that a team is interdependent for overall performance. The *Concise Oxford Dictionary* defines team work as 'combined effort, organized co-operation'. A group heading towards a common objective will perform best when it is motivated as a team. Team motivation is determined by how well the team members' needs and requirements are met by the team.

In the sales world, sales leaders must understand the difference between a sales team and a sales force. In some companies, it is essential to create a sales team that shares information and works collectively to achieve given criteria and sales results. Individuals should then be rewarded as a team and share in the commission and bonuses. In other sales environments, a sales force in which the individual succeeds or fails upon his or her own actions is necessary. In such an environment, individuals are rewarded for their individual performance. In the sporting world, we acclaim teams and we praise team spirit. If only managers and supervisors in the business community applied the same principles. Understanding the principles that exist in the sporting world, it would be truly amazing to see the results that could be achieved.

PRINCIPLES OF TEAM MOTIVATION

So let's now look at some of those principles that can be applied both socially and commercially and let begin by stressing the importance of this expression: 'The climate must be right.' This is a principle that, of course, applies not only to motivating yourself, but also to turning a group into a team. In order for people to be motivated and happy in their work, there are five common sense principles to be followed.

1. They should be capable

People must be capable of carrying out the job, task or position that they are given. We have all heard the expression: 'A square peg in a round hole.' In the sales world, it is often considered essential that in order to be a sales manager one has to be a good salesperson. This is true, but it does not mean that a good salesperson will necessarily be a good sales manager. Somebody who is not a good salesperson cna never be a good sales manager. The team of sales people was led by a sales manager who was obviously the 'square peg in the round hole'. His title should have been 'sales administration manager', which was where his skill, talents, confidence and enthusiasm really lay. The team of people were suffering as well inasmuch as the team was at the bottom of the league table of 12 regions. The sales manager had a very introverted personality, had never really achieved any sales success and was much more comfortable with a computer than with people. He should never have been put into the position of sales manager or a leader of people.

2. They must be fit for it

Yes, people should be able, through training and through personal development programmes, to be fit for the part they have to play in their team. But let also touch on another of the old clichés: 'You can take a horse to water, but you can't make it drink.' If the individual does not want to be trained or does not want the post that they have been given, they will never become fit for it.

3. They must not overindulged

For people to be happy in their work, they should not do too much of it. They must get the balance right. We all know the expression: 'All work and no play makes Jack a very dull boy.' It also produces staleness in performance if people are not getting a contrast of activities in their lives. Contrast is absolutely essential in maintaining maximum enthusiasm and effectiveness.

4. They must experience success

For individuals in a team to achieve success, they must be happy and that happiness can be developed through the enjoyment of the success feeling.

Here we are again mentioning that law of success that says: seeing ourselves progressing motivates us.

5. They must have the right attitude

We must remember that we are looking at ideas that can apply equally to a team at work, at play, or engaged in any other activity. When people are at play, following a social hobby or charitable activity, they are less likely to take offence at the four-letter word—work. Work is something we do not usually do without reward, and the reward for the majority of people is money. So the example of people being happy to work when at play shows that it is a person's attitude towards work that is so important. If people would accept this, then in most cases, the more successful they will be at their work, the more rewards they will receive. This in turn can only mean greater enjoyment when they are away from their work at weekends, evenings and holidays.

CREATING THE TEAM ENVIRONMENT

The climate must be right. Here are a further 11 key tips that create the right environment for the team to become naturally self-motivated. This surely is one of the great principles of good motivational leadership, that it is not something that is imposed or forced, but is a natural positive climate for motivational expression.

1. Positive working conditions

What this means is that the equipment, tools and systems that team members are required to use do, in fact, actually work. Every one of us has experienced at some time the frustration of faulty equipment or systems. If it remains unrepaired then, undoubtedly, demotivation sets in. Working conditions should, of course, be clean and comfortable. People should be proud of the place in which they work—and the balance here is crucial.

2. Team players

All members of a team must be team players and it is often worthwhile making the effort to ensure this is the case by using personality profiling or psychometric testing. Sometimes, tough decisions have to be taken in replacing people who are not team players. Rest assured, others within the team will understand when they are on the receiving end of a non-team player.

3. The culture of priorities

Remember the greatest management principal: *Whatever you reward, you will get more of.* For a motivated team, therefore, it is essential that all members of the team know what their individual priorities are in working towards the team's objective.

What does the manager reward or recognize? Let's look at some examples:

— Do people get rewarded who look busy and work long hours rather than those who get results?

— Are demands made for quality work, but unrealistic deadlines set?

— Is company loyalty demanded and talked about, but with no offer of job security?

— Are people given large budget increases after exhausting their resources, yet frugality demanded?

— Are people frightened to try something different because of fear of chastisement when what is really needed is creative input?

— Is teamwork demanded, yet one member of a team played off against another?

The culture of priorities is very much linked with the behaviour that is expected. People will always behave the way the reward mechanism has trained them.

4. A common goal

There must be a common goal, an objective or even a cause to fight for. It is utterly impossible to motivate a team of people without one of these three things. It is no good imposing a goal that stimulates the manager, but does not interest the participants. This leads on to the importance of creating the goal by a collective decision-making process. This is really plain common sense, but it is staggering how many companies and organizations do not seem to adhere to this principle.

It is possible to create excellent incentive programmes or to organize and present some great motivational seminars. Or you could go to the other extreme of motivation–which is to threaten people with the sack. But that can never be as successful as getting people involved and genuinely participating. Goals that people have some responsibility for setting are much more likely to be achieved than those that are imposed. And common goals do become effective motivators. In creating a common goal, the motivator must also create the stimulation of new goals from time to time.

5. Have a vision

Mission statements were a must, and were no doubt dreamt up by some management consultant. They have now proved to be completely ineffectual. Mission statements were of course created with the belief that it would be of benefit for the staff and for their customers. Most organizations attempted to get their employees to help develop the company's mission. Eventually these wordy, virtuous statements were produced and framed in the entrance lobby. Hardly anybody could actually recall what the statement was. It was one of these appalling fads that were absolutely useless but nevertheless took up hours of creative time.

6. Maintain a high energy level

People are naturally more motivated when they are busy. They very rarely suffer from body fatigue, but they do suffer, as we have already discussed, from mental fatigue—stress. However, working really hard while avoiding stress is almost unheard of as a cause of medical complaint.

7. Remember the individual

Significance of the individual is still important, even though people are part of a team.

A team is a number of individuals who are interdependent on their overall performance, but who are still individuals in their own right. They must individually feel that their treatment is fair and just. They must individually feel that they are recognized for their contribution. They must individually feel that the part they play contributes towards the goal or the achievement. They must individually have the loyalty and respect of the manager and their colleagues.

While on the subject of loyalty and respect, let's be realistic: this is something that is learnt in life and should never be demanded or expected.

8. Team identity

Have you noticed how people are so willing to wear sweat-shirts and T-shirts that are emblazoned with the name of their sporting team? It is one of the principles of motivation that we talked about earlier: group belonging motivates. So as a manager, look at every possibility of creating your team's identity.

9. Share success

Team members must be able to share in the rewards of success. You will undoubtedly have noticed at the football World Cup Final how the captain of the team is presented with the cup, which is duly kissed and held aloft, but is then passed to every member of the team, and how all team members get their own winner's medal, not just the captain or the manager.

10. The positive team

How do the team members communicate with each other? Is it positive or is it negative? Where it is practical, team bonding can be created by the team experiencing activities outside the daily routine of work. Activity weekends, attending courses as a group and team competitions are all very worthwhile. When there is a situation created in which individuals can care for and support each other, it can contribute to a more motivated unit. If it is negative, the one absolute certainty is that the team will become an unproductive team.

It is very much the responsibility of the manager or leader to prevent negative communication spreading infectiously.

Most effective managers teach and train people on the subject of the positive and the negative. We are all aware of the expression: 'The bad apple in the barrel can pollute all the others.' And so it is with a team of people. It only takes one person to become truly negative for the remainder of that team to gradually become negative as well. And a negative team is most certainly not a motivated team.

TIPS FOR EFFECTIVE TEAM MOTIVATION

It is so worthwhile for employees to go away as a group. No doubt you have experienced this at some stage when you have been on a course with others. It is common that they are complete strangers prior to the course, but at the end of it, isn't it amazing how you all become more drawn together! So by taking your team away either for training, discussion or even for a leisure trip, you will draw them closer together.

These occasions do not have to be expensive if the budgets are tight. In its simplest form, the trip can be a quick drink one evening after work or a visit to a restaurant or theatre. Then there are the more glamorous three- or four-day outward-bound-type courses. However, a word of warning here for all managers and leaders. The clichéd expression 'Familiarity breeds contempt' is unfortunately all too accurate. So as a manager you must always be prepared to keep a certain amount of distance between yourself and your team. Once employees or team members see or experience your own weaknesses, you will most certainly lose some of their respect. We all have our own weaknesses. It is essential, therefore, that, with the enormous responsibility any leader or manager carries, while with their team they are always on duty—or as they say in the military, 'on parade'.

Some tips for effective team motivation are as follows:

— The team's objective should well align and synchronize with the team members needs and requirements.

— Give in written the team's mission and ensure that all understand it (as mission is a foundation based on which the team performs).

— For maintaining motivation, the team should be given challenges (which must be difficult but achievable) consistently.

— Giving a team responsibility accompanied by authority can also be a good motivator for the team to perform.

— The team should be provided with growth opportunities. The team's motivation level is high when the team members feel that they are being promoted, their skills and competencies are being enhanced, and they are learning new things consistently.

— Effective and true leaders can develop environment for the team to motivate itself. They provide spur for self-actualization behaviours of team members.

— Devote quality/productive time to your team. Have an optimistic and good relation with your team members. This will make you more acquainted with them and you can get knowledge of how well they are performing their job. Welcome their views and ideas as they may be fruitful and it will also boost their morale.

— Motivation is all about empowerment. The skills and competencies of the team members should be fully utilized. Empowering the team members makes them accountable for their own actions.

— Provide feedback to the team consistently. Become their mentor. Give the team recognition for good and outstanding performance. Give the team a constructive and not negative feedback.

— Discover and offset the factors which discourage team spirit such as too many conflicts, lethargy, team members' escape from responsibilities, lack of job satisfaction, etc.

10

INCENTIVE MOTIVATION

Incentive is an act or promise for greater action. It is also called as a stimulus to greater action. Incentives are something which are given in addition to wagers. It means additional remuneration or benefit to an employee in recognition of achievement or better work. Incentives provide a spur or zeal in the employees for better performance. It is a natural thing that nobody acts without a purpose behind. Therefore, a hope for a reward is a powerful incentive to motivate employees. Besides monetary incentive, there are some other stimuli which can drive a person to better. This will include job satisfaction, job security, job promotion, and pride for accomplishment. Therefore, incentives really can sometimes work to accomplish the goals of a concern. The need of incentives can be many:

— To increase productivity,

— To drive or arouse a stimulus work,

— To enhance commitment in work performance,

— To psychologically satisfy a person which leads to job satisfaction,

— To shape the behaviour or outlook of subordinate towards work,

- To inculcate zeal and enthusiasm towards work,
- To get the maximum of their capabilities so that they are exploited and utilized maximally.

CATEGORIES OF INCENTIVES

Therefore, management has to offer the following two categories of incentives to motivate employees:

Monetary Incentives

Those incentives which satisfy the subordinates by providing them rewards in terms of rupees. Money has been recognized as a chief source of satisfying the needs of people. Money is also helpful to satisfy the social needs by possessing various material items. Therefore, money not only satisfies psychological needs but also the security and social needs. Therefore, in many factories, various wage plans and bonus schemes are introduced to motivate and stimulate the people to work.

Non-monetary Incentives

Besides the monetary incentives, there are certain non-financial incentives which can satisfy the ego and self-actualization needs of employees. The incentives which cannot be measured in terms of money are under the category of "Non- monetary incentives". Whenever a manager has to satisfy the psychological needs of the subordinates, he makes use of non-financial incentives.

Non-financial incentives can be of the following types:

Security of Service

Job security is an incentive which provides great motivation to employees. If his job is secured, he will put maximum efforts to achieve the objectives of the enterprise. This also helps since he is very far off from mental tension and he can give his best to the enterprise.

Praise or Recognition

The praise or recognition is another non-financial incentive which satisfies the ego needs of the employees. Sometimes praise becomes more effective than any other incentive. The employees will respond more to praise and try to give the best of their abilities to a concern.

Suggestion Scheme

The organization should look forward to taking suggestions and inviting suggestion schemes from the subordinates. This inculcates a spirit of participation in the employees. This can be done by publishing various articles written by employees to improve the work environment which can be published in various magazines of the company. This also is helpful to motivate the employees to feel important and they can also be in search for innovative methods which can be applied for better work methods. This ultimately helps in growing a concern and adapting new methods of operations.

Job Enrichment

Job enrichment is another non-monetary incentive in which the job of a worker can be enriched. This can be done by increasing his responsibilities, giving him an important designation, increasing the content and nature of the work. This way efficient worker can get challenging jobs in which they can prove their worth. This also helps in the greatest motivation of the efficient employees.

Promotion Opportunities

Promotion is an effective tool to increase the spirit to work in a concern. If the employees are provided opportunities for the advancement and growth, they feel satisfied and contented and they become more committed to the organization.

The above non-financial tools can be framed effectively by giving due concentration to the role of employees. A combination of financial and non-financial incentives help together in bringing motivation and zeal to work in a concern.

Positive Incentives

Positive incentives are those incentives which provide a positive assurance for fulfilling the needs and wants. Positive incentives generally have an optimistic attitude behind and they are generally given to satisfy the psychological requirements of employees. For example, promotion, praise, recognition, perks and allowances, etc. It is positive by nature.

Negative Incentives

Negative incentives are those whose purpose is to correct the mistakes or defaults of employees. The purpose is to rectify mistakes in order to get effective results. Negative incentive is generally resorted to when positive incentive does not works and a psychological set back has to be given to employees. It is negative by nature. For example- demotion, transfer, fines, penalties.

POWER OF AN INCENTIVE

It is quite extraordinary how the majority of people find a balance in their employer–employee relationship during their working lives. Many people work just hard enough so they don't get fired and in return their employer pays them just enough so that they don't leave. It is on this sort of happy or unhappy basis that life proceeds.

But, when the happiness and enjoyment factor is high on both sides, success is inevitable.

A successful incentive programme will not only increase profits, but can also inspire staff loyalty and raise morale. Most people seem to go to work to do a reasonable job, but not an exceptional one.

Yet these same people will devote many hours to hobbies and charities without any monetary reward and do an exceptional job. What they do get, however, is recognition.

Some of us have friends or colleagues who devote enormous amounts of energy and time to organizations such as the Round Table or Rotary International. We also have friends who have a greater interest in their extracurricular activities than they have in their work.

As with everything else, over-indulgence can become destructive. The recognition can almost become like a drug.

If such people were to apply the same effort to their work practice, untold rewards could be reaped.

Many managers make the mistake of thinking that money is the prime motivational requirement. Yet these same managers may be promoted to positions with monetary reward packages lower than those of some of their employees.

Recognition

Let us now concentratethoughts on the importance of

recognition and what it really means. It is the most powerful incentive for motivation. In it simplest form, recognition can be a simple 'thank you'. This, of course, is best and most effectively given in public, where other workmates or colleagues can hear that gratitude being expressed. We all know the extraordinary lengths people will go to in order to gain some recognition. How people love to appear on TV, on the radio, to have their photograph in the local paper. In the United Kingdom there is still incredible interest and prestige in the Honours List. Nearly every profession has some method of recognizing its outstanding performers–the most obvious are the Oscar nominations and the Emmy awards. Almost every profession or business organization has some national award scheme.

In the armed services, medals are awarded. In the sporting world, the winner is placed on the highest platform.

So, accepting the power of recognition, let's now go through a few examples that can be used in the business world. For those of you who are commercially minded, you will be pleased to hear it is the cheapest and most cost effective of all forms of incentive.

Cost-effective Incentives

Sales managers should circulate lists showing the sales results of each individual in their sales team. In very large sales organizations this can be broken down into league tables and when these tables are published, every individual will look for their own name first. Inevitably, the only people who are likely to object to this will be those at the bottom of the list or league. Certificates of achievement can be awarded, and these are best presented already framed. These certificates do get hung. They also act as an ongoing reminder of achievement.

In all business and commerce operations, people can be motivated by a change of job title. This is sometimes the only way of preventing the loss of an otherwise high-performing individual. Think up a new or more prestigious title.

For example, these are some of the titles that people have changed themselves:

— Groom has been changed to equine technician.

— A rat catcher to a pest control officer.

— A traveller to a sales executive.

— A housewife to a home executive.

If you can't think what to call somebody, and you really don't know what they do, how about Vice President?!

Wall plaques can be presented as well as the traditional cups and trophies. No doubt you will have seen in some organizations that people are given recognition through the tie that they wear; in others, it is in the car that they drive. In yet another, people are given named parking places for their vehicles. Dangerous because this really can become extremely divisive. In some businesses, some people are allowed to enter and leave by a different door and, yet again, in other companies, people's status is judged by the size of the budget they are responsible for. All of these examples are getting the principles of recognition dangerously wrong. First, because they divide, and secondly because you get more of what you reward. In business, success does not come from how much you spend, but how much you earn.

Recognition can also be given if one has an in-house magazine, newsletter or e-mail, in which, wherever possible, a photograph of the high-performing individual should be included. People will always look at the photo graphs first. The most effective managers and leaders will always give the recognition and make the presentations in public, but will follow this up with a personal congratulatory letter. As we all know, these letters never end up in a wastepaper basket.

Try to Remember Names

Let's now change thinking for a minute or two towards other forms that recognition can take. The sweetest sound in the English language is the sound of your own name. The most senior executive who, while on the shop floor, knows the names of all his employees, and perhaps even their partners' names and some other personal details, will be held in great reverence by the workforce. Not all of us are gifted with brilliant memories, but a little bit of planning and preparation and maybe even briefing by junior managers can overcome a lapse in memory. Remembering people's birthdays and anniversaries is another great form of recognition.

Money

Let us now move on to the third great reward: money.

Money, as we have already said, is not an incentive unless a person has an insufficient amount coming in for his or her immediate requirements. Therefore, if money is to be used as an incentive, it has to be of considerable quantity. Another trouble with using money as an incentive is that it can be spent on household bills, which will leave no lasting advancement for the individual. Now let's get this into perspective. More and more companies are showing, by getting people involved with share ownership and an interest in the overall profitability of their company, the successes that can be achieved.

Charitable giving is a great example of this point. It is extremely important for charitable collections to give maximum recognition and 'thank yous' to people for their contributions to charitable work. Very few major donations are given anonymously. In past decades, credit cards were almost a status symbol, and the card companies were forever thinking up more creative ways not only to get people to pay for the card subscription, but also to spend more. So Gold Cards were created, followed by Platinum, followed by Super Platinum and so on.

But as with so many status symbols, not only is there a price to pay, but they lose their glamour as people become more aware and more logical. Nevertheless, there will always be new status symbols. For example, expensive holidays and second homes can perhaps now be classified as such.

INCENTIVE CONTESTS

Let us now have a look at the rules and principles of setting up an incentive programme within an organization i.e., a contest. Let first of all establish a concept–all contests that are organized and run successfully are self-financing and do not become a cost. They are paid for not by those who win but by those who do not win, and have raised their level of performance in attempting to win. Such people will also spur others to greater levels of achievement.

Five Basic Rules

Break these five basic rules and your contest will almost certainly not be a success. It will approach a contest or an incentive programme with some scepticism, either because you have been on the receiving end of one that demotivated you or because you have put one into practice that was a complete flop.

1. Contests that work are those in which everyone has a chance to win. If they do not have that chance, they will not even try. This is the first reason why a contest might not work.

   The second reason is even more dangerous: the contest can work from the point of view of getting people striving for a goal, but after its completion it might destroy future altitudes towards contests. This can be shown using the example of a raffle-type contest in the sales world, where each sale that takes place qualifies the salesperson for a raffle ticket. The theory is that the more sales made, the more chances of winning a prize. At the end of the qualifying period, the raffle is drawn and it can happen that one of the lowest-performing salespeople wins first prize because, as we all know, a raffle is chance, not luck. This can cause massive demotivation in those who have really striven to achieve.

2. Long-term contests are of little value if one is attempting to increase business immediately. This is not to say that long-term contests are of no value—they are. Many organizations have their annual awards: salesperson of the year, manager of the year, etc. They are incredibly important and should always be in existence.

   But if one wants an immediate uplift or an instant change of results, the maximum time the contest should run is three months. For those of you who have run longer-term contests, no doubt you will have found that you achieved the increased performance in the month before the contest was due to close. So it is therefore advisable that if you organize a long-term contest, you have a secondary shorter-term contest running alongside it.

Having said that, you should ideally only have one contest running at any one time. The long-term or secondary contests do not attract the continual attention or publicity that the short-term contest does. Never have two short-term contests running concurrently. It is the old sales principal—you can only ever sell one product at a time.

3. Whenever you are constructing a contest, ask yourself: 'What do we want to achieve with this?' This may sound like common sense, but it is quite amazing how few people do ask themselves this question. Let remind you once again of the greatest management principle in the world—you will get more of what you reward.

4. Prizes, as we have already said, should not be in money but in some tangible form. The prizes that one can give can range from the engraved crystal glass through to the Christmas hamper; bottles of wine to a selection from a pre-prepared catalogue of gifts. There are many excellent companies that will put together a superb catalogue of prizes or gifts. Some of these do, of course, relate to a points structure very similar to the ones we have all experienced, from supermarket reward card schemes.

The finest and most effective of all prizes is travel and time off. From weekends away to visits to exotic places around the world. But if you are ever going to use travel or holidays as an incentive, there should always be a pair of tickets. This will maximize its effect, gain fuller support and mean greater effort towards increased performance. What is wrong with a culture (providing it has no impact on others) in which, when people have finished and completed all their allocated or expected work, they can go home? We still retain the culture of paying people for the hours, not for what they do within those hours. But even if you can't change this culture, you can give people a half-day or a day off when they have achieved something beyond your expectations.

You can imagine the demotivation it could cause at home if, for example, a weekend in Amsterdam or a two-week holiday in the Seychelles were available for only one person! The incentive of a pair of tickets, however, would draw that family or partnership together–one encouraging the other, both sharing the reward.

5. Contests must set the following three questions, and unless they are readily and easily answered, your contest will be unworkable:

   — Exactly what do I have to do?

   — Exactly what do I get?

   — By when?

MANAGING THE INCENTIVE SCHEME

Having constructed your incentive programme or contest based solidly around the above rules, the following stages must be observed to maximize its eventual success. All contests should be totally cost effective and paid for by enhanced profits made from the increase in performance. But contests must be sold to the participants, so the motivated manager should follow the structure below in announcing the programme to the participants.

Stage 1

Tell them what the prize(s) are. Have pictures or samples available and follow this up by giving every participant either a brochure or a photograph of the prizes.

Stage 2

Now tell them what they have to do in order to achieve these prizes and again make sure that this is fair, that everybody has a chance to participate and that they are also given clear and precise details.

Stage 3

Tell them when the contest starts and when it finishes. Again, be realistic here. Never announce your contest too early, as your high achievers or most ambitious people will hold back business until the qualifying start of the contest.

Stage 4

Finally, sell it and sell it again. This is where another mistake often occurs when people run incentive programmes. They spend a lot of effort putting it all together, maybe even having a grand conference to launch it, and then it is very rarely talked about or promoted until its conclusion when the results are announced.

Incentives do work, but please give your incentive programme the maximum chance of success by continual promotion, by constantly letting the participants know how far they are from the various prizes or stages on offer. And if you are the manager running the contest, continually talk about it to your people. Each time you speak to the people who are involved in the contest, mention it, sell it and tell them how they are doing. This can be done through face-to-face meetings, e-mail or on the telephone.

Success or Failure

Let now give you an example of a contest where people can successfully compete with each other even though they are working on the proverbial 'unlevel playing field'. This is again based upon sales achievement, but the principles can, of course, be applied to other tasks and activities.

In this simple example, we have six people: Rohit, Mannu, Tiwari, J.P., Harish and Billo. The sales manager gets together privately with each one and agrees a target for the three-month period.

	Agreed target
Rohit	60
Mannu	70
Tiwari	30
J.P.	40
Harish	60
Billo.	80

The prizes to be awarded are as follows:
— First prize to the person who achieves the greatest overall number of sales.
— A prize for each person who achieves exactly what they have agreed to do.
— A prize equal to the first prize for the person who gets the greatest percentage above their target.

Looking at winners, we see that Mannu got the top prize for selling the most, but Harish got the other top prize for having the greatest percentage increase. We see that Tiwari, who might otherwise have never been able to win a prize, was awarded his because he did exactly what he said he would do.

	Agreed target	*Sales results*
Rohit	60	58
Mannu	70	70
Tiwari	30	30
J.P.	40	38
Harish	60	68
Billo.	80	69

This is an example, in its simplest form, of a contest where everybody has a chance to win.

 ❖❖❖

11

MOTIVATION THROUGH EFFECTIVE COMMUNICATION

Communication is the heart and soul of motivating employees. Employees are demotivated when they are unsure of manager expectations and priorities. They're motivated when managers provide clear expectations, instructions, information, and time frames, creating within the employees a sense of security, respect, power, and control in their jobs. Furthermore, managers need to communicate encouragement during the process as well as acknowledgement and appreciation upon achievement of outcomes.

People are said to judge leaders more by what they do than by what they say. But it is actually what leaders express through either verbal or written communication that will make the difference to how they will be judged. Perhaps the most major cause of strife and problems throughout the world is breakdown in communications. This can often be as simple as a misunderstanding.

Unfortunately, many supervisors and managers don't believe that it is necessary to keep people informed. They operate with the attitude that people have jobs to do and ought to get on and do them—and not waste time talking.

167

This is a very short-sighted view. Management activity in any organization cannot take place without full and open two-way communications. That means speaking as well as listening.

The first and possibly the most important rule of communication is to make clear the message being communicated. Communication will never have the desired effect if the other person doesn't comprehend the meaning. No manager can get the desired results through an incomplete or misunderstood message. A successful motivated manager understand and reads people's body language. Less than 10 per cent of all communication skills are verbal. So the real art of communication is the ability to convey information or a message from one person to another with absolute clarity.

Communication is a two-way process, giving the communicator the opportunity to respond to messages as well as give them. Any manager who can't or won't communicate well will simply never be able to do a good job or get good results.

IMPACT OF EFFECTIVE COMMUNICATION ON MOTIVATIONAL CLIMATE

Supervisors, top executives and managers spend most of their time communicating to others—from step-by-step tasks to overall company vision. The most effective communicators not only help workers carry out day-to-day tasks but inspire staff to challenge themselves and each other to outstanding performance.

Clued-in Workers

Employees respond more enthusiastically to leadership they feel confident in. Executives build employee confidence in leadership's capability by helping employees to understand the company's general strategy and to identify their particular contribution to executing it. Managers don't just deliver marching orders; they explain how the tactics help the team and total company complete the assigned mission.

Executive Leadership

Different company cultures require different leadership styles to effectively communicate to the workforce and motivate it to accomplish their aims. Two primary styles work well for the executive level as leaders chart a course for their business. Executives can employ a structural style that concentrates on implementing or adapting strategy to fit the organization's makeup, experimenting with the general environment for improvements. Or they can draw a vision for the company with images that capture employees' imaginations, the way a director stages scenes and actors in a film.

Middle Management Rapport

Just as executives can exploit different communication styles to shape a company's vision, managers can adapt their interaction style to motivate diverse departments or teams. Managers can adopt a strategy that focuses on the nature of power, linking coalitions together and negotiating among stakeholders to reach goals by appealing to worker's self interest, answering the questions "what's in it for me?" Or managers can concentrate on the individual, searching for ways to support an employee's professional development, motivating staff at all levels to greater contributions.

Balancing Act

Effectual leadership must strike a balance between freedom and discipline when motivating staff. This can be a moving target, as work situations continually evolve. Managers grapple with aligning employee's individual ambitions with the organizations' objectives, while employees may struggle with fitting in to a company that seems to be continuously changing, while taking responsibility for the company's success. Effective communication, with managers taking the lead, fosters trust within the workforce, which leads to a more compelling exchange of ideas, helps staff to embrace more responsibility, and encourages management to stretch for higher targets.

Effective Communication

Managers must communicate effectively to enable opinion and comment and encourage staff to generate ideas, reach decisions or even make mistakes. This safe haven will build consensus and a sense of ownership among the workforce. Leaders can destroy trust if they develop a reputation for quashing criticism or shooting the messenger. They also can stifle motivation with an authoritarian stance on decisions instead of developing a sense of accord within teams by encouraging input to reach resolution of challenges or choices that affect the team's effort and goals.

COMMUNICATING VIA TELEPHONE

Let's begin with perhaps the most widely used tool of communication—the telephone. How do you and I speak to friends, colleagues and employees over the phone?

Take first of all the incoming phone call. When you answer the phone, sound positive and enthusiastic. When they announce their name, sound even more pleased that they are phoning you. In other words, make them feel good, make them feel important.

'How nice to hear you.'

'I am so glad you phoned.'

'It's great to hear from you.'

But always say it with a smile—it's amazing how these words sound more genuine and seem to come out more effectively when uttered by lips shaped to a smile!

Now consider the phone calls that you have to make. Plan and decide exactly what you would like to say. Again, sound positive, sound enthusiastic. If you are a manager communicating with your people, your words are extremely important. So having commenced with the courtesy or the pleasantry, 'How are you?', switch straight into the purpose of your call. A successful sales manager, having made a brief courteous enquiry, will then ask after his or her salesperson's performance. But don't do what some managers do, namely talk about almost everything else rather than get to the point of the call. They enquire first about such mundane topics as what is in the news. Get to the point. What is important to you also becomes important to your people.

Many supervisors and managers use e-mail as a major tool of communication and may only meet face-to-face perhaps at a weekly or monthly meeting. The telephone becomes secondary. In such cases the telephone communication takes on an even greater importance. It becomes an opportunity to re-motivate and re-enthuse. The manager should always plan on having some good news to pass on down the line. Managers must urgently take on board this very important concept—e-mail is not a management tool and is only of real value for the exchange of important information. To communicate more effectively, don't use e-mail; use the telephone. The manager should keep staff well informed of news, developments and all changes and opportunities. Remember the expression 'Let them hear it from the horse's mouth.'

While on the subject of the telephone, always try to take your incoming calls: you should never be too busy. Avoid being endlessly tied up in meetings. Also, if you are absent from the office, make sure that useless information is not being passed out.

At the end of every telephone call, see if you can leave the other person thinking 'I am glad I spoke to you today.' The telephone is an opportunity to motivate and inspire, so use it well!

FACE-TO-FACE MEETINGS

How do people arrive at the office first thing in the morning? How do managers and supervisors greet their employees? What sort of people you want to have working with you — positive, enthusiastic, dedicated, 'raring to go' types? Of course you do. In which case, change must start with you.

First greetings in the morning are so important. And just as important as what we say is appearance and body language.

Enthusiasm is infectious, so always have a positive message. Become a carrier of good news. Be consistent and not moody. People are much more secure under a management style that is consistent. And, above everything else, keep problems away from those who they do not concern. Managers and leaders, apart from the recognition they get, normally earn more, and for this they have a greater responsibility. Within this greater responsibility they have problems that require solving, solutions that they have to find. Only weak managers will dump their worries and problems on their teams. Don't get your people worrying about your worries. It is more than likely that they cannot help, and they should not be asked to solve your problems anyhow.

RUMOUR-MONGERING CAUSES STRIFE

In most organizations strife is often caused through rumours. Try to recall the last rumour that did the rounds in your organization. Just how true or how distorted was it? How destructive was it?

Most rumours appear to be fairly harmless, but they can reduce morale and damage productivity. Now, we can't alter human nature or prevent people from inventing rumours, listening to them, embellishing them or passing them on. But what we can all do is prevent the conditions that invite rumours. Surely the condition that encourages rumours more than any other is secrecy, as it only makes people wonder, imagine and gossip. The more somebody tries to keep a secret, the more interesting it must be. Therefore, the more news you can give people, the less tendency they will have to invent their own.

We all need to know what is going on in the organization of which we are part. People are never going to stop thinking and talking about things that affect them—their jobs and their livelihood—and the less factual information there is, the greater the spread of misinformation will be. So before you decide to keep something really secret, think first: 'Is it really necessary?' Good managers avoid secrecy about their jobs and work practices. They pass on all the information that they can. They make themselves available to answer questions and discuss issues with their people.

WRITTEN COMMUNICATION

Breakdown of communication is the major cause of most of the world's strife. But there is one segment within this vast subject area that carries a significant amount of responsibility for the misery caused. This is *written* communication. It is the most dangerous form of communication. Whenever words go on to paper in the form of letters, memos, faxes or e-mails—watch out.

More strikes and industrial problems within companies have been caused by the written word than by any other single factor. The written word in most cases will be read negatively. It is open for people to interpret in their own way the emphasis on certain words. More can be read into a written letter than is ever actually intended. Never write anything other than a positive congratulatory communication. Or if it is for the purpose of exchanging information, make sure it is very factual and specific. If you get a letter from a superior that is critical about smoothing you have been doing, are you motivated or demotivated? We all know the answer! Whether the criticism was justified or not has little to do with it. You will be demotivated. Surely this is not the purpose of the letter.

If you have to write a letter to any of your people, make sure that it is good news. If you have bad news or you need to criticize somebody, tell them face to face, or at least over the phone so they have a chance to respond. The matter can be discussed, dealt with and cleared up.

Memos and E-mails

Internal memos and e-mails can also be very destructive. Some managers resort to memos or e-mails rather than to more direct communication. Apart from taking up time, a critical memo or e-mail sent to another person can cause even greater stress, as the recipient will wonder who else has seen the memo into the e-mail.

Any manager who uses only written communication should not be in a position of supervising or managing others. The best use of the written word is the clear exchange of information.

MOTIVATIONAL CRITICISM

People who have a responsibility to supervise have a great number of things they have to control. Not the least of these is their own personal feelings towards their subordinates. Managers and supervisors are, of course, human, and they do have their own likes and dislikes just like everyone else. An effective and motivated manager will, however, make sure that their feelings about their subordinates do not show. It is quite obvious that performance will suffer if an employee should feel that their immediate boss doesn't like them, treats them unjustly or favours somebody else. From time to time it is necessary to get a person back on the rails or criticize them in order to get the performance and the results that you deserve.

Motivational criticism should not be related to a personal like or dislike. It should primarily be because of a feeling of concern. Also, it is a manager's duty to guide his employees not only towards performance that keeps them in their job, but performance that helps them to achieve their goals—and, of course, maintains the team spirit. The purpose of the criticism is not and should never be to destroy, but to build.

The points that the manager should discuss must be constructive and not destructive. It takes very little brains to find fault. It takes a lot more brains to find a better way of doing something. It's all very well if the manager knows what he wants to communicate, but he is communicating with another person, and that person also has the wonderful asset of the human brain. Therefore, in order to get the message across, you have to make sure that you haven't got a closed mind when communicating. At the commencement of the meeting, you must open up the other person's mind so that it becomes receptive to you. The person must be able to listen, take in, discuss and then react to the message that you are giving.

In many cases, a manager is forced into criticizing an employee because of actions that have been immensely irritating. Sometimes an employee acts irresponsibly and—even worse—with the intention of breaking some rule or acceptable work practice. Some managers lose their temper and react immediately. In a state of fury, they criticize the subordinate. Don't do it—it does occasionally work, but it invariably destroys relationships, and will cause a dramatic loss of respect.

Successful Motivational Criticism

Let's now run through the nine stages of successful motivational criticism:

Stage 1

Pick your time carefully. It can be very upsetting for a person to be criticized, maybe even over a minor mistake, when they are just about to tackle an important job.

Is it right to criticize someone on a Friday evening—just before they are going home for the weekend—when they will have little chance of putting right the points you have raised?

Stage 2

Your discussion must be in complete privacy. You know the rule—praise in public, chastise in private.

Under no circumstances whatsoever should anybody, either colleague, subordinate or superior, be able to overhear or oversee your discussion. This is common sense, but it is a mistake that so many managers make, and then they wonder why they get a hostile reaction. In most cases, this hostility is caused by the person who is being criticized not really listening but worrying about what their colleagues will be thinking. This causes them to put up a fight, again for the benefit of the listeners. It is like playing to the gallery.

Stage 3

Before you mention the constructive points of criticism, make the person receptive to you; this is very simply done by letting the other person know that you do appreciate them and by listing all the good things that they do.This can be complimentary and the good manager looks to catch people doing things right. So this first stage, to a certain extent, is motivational, but it makes the person prepared and open minded enough to listen and discuss the problems in a reasonable fashion. Tell them their good points, remind them of their successes and achievements. Everybody has some.

Stage 4

Look the person in the eyes. The manager who is unable to look the other person in the face loses credibility and the strength of the message suffers. Some people look out of the window or at their feet and consequently they weaken dramatically what they have to say.

Stage 5

Be strictly truthful. This is not to imply that managers tend to tell lies. But what does often happen is that they have difficulty in 'telling it the way it is'. They believe that their subordinate has sufficient imagination to interpret a vague message. They rely too much on innuendo, hoping that the other person gets the point without actually saying what the point is.

So tell it the way it is. Be specific. And if it does relate to a personal characteristic–for example, where the person's appearance is letting them down–a caring manager will point this out.

We've all heard the expression that it is only a real friend who will tell you the truth; so it should be with a good, caring and motivated manager.

Stage 6

Try not to criticize a person, but do criticize the person's actions. One must be very careful not to criticize a person in what one can describe as the area of 'values and beliefs'.

There are occasions when, by criticizing behaviour, one has to mention the cause, as we discussed in the previous stage. But this is the crux of the communication process: *behaviour* leads to the results that one wants to change or improve, and it is in this area that one must be absolutely specific and clear.

Stage 7

Having discussed the various points that are targets of criticism, the manager must then build that person up again. This is easily and effectively done by reaffirming their good points. Again, spell these out.

Let's remember the purpose of criticism. You want to send the individual out of the meeting having listened to and accepted the criticism, but also saying to themselves 'I am going to put right what was wrong', and with the respect and loyalty between the two parties still intact.

The purpose of criticism is not to destroy the confidence, self-image and self-belief of the other person. It is to build on in the future.

Stage 8

The date of the review is important, as it shows the commitment of the manager to follow through his criticism, as well as giving a goal for the subordinate to aim towards.

Stage 9

The final stage is, of course, the praise that the manager should give when the criticized person gets it right.

Whatever you reward, you get more of. That praise is a prize in the reward stakes.

Problems of Dismissal

Just before we leave the subject of criticism, the motivated manager will unfortunately, from time to time, have to dismiss an employee.

Once that decision has been taken, it should not be delayed. In most cases, to preserve the team the departure should happen as speedily as possible. There are, of course, exceptions to this rule in which people can work out a period of notice. In most cases, this is extremely dangerous and will be demotivational to the remainder of the team. It is therefore better for everybody concerned that, when that decision has been taken, the person concerned leaves the company immediately.

Any manager obviously hates having to tell an employee that their services are no longer required. Nevertheless, it is one of the burdens and responsibilities for which managers are duly rewarded.

When firing another individual, the manager should never destroy them. A manager should never set out to break down their self-image, confidence or self-belief. If the decision to dismiss has been taken, it is right to give justifiable, fair and logical reasons, so you have to communicate the truth. In some cases, however, you do not have to tell the whole truth. If the individual does get angry or uptight, it really doesn't matter to the manager. Treat it as a 'So what?' exercise. Far better that that person goes out feeling angry, but with their attitude, beliefs and confidence intact so that they can go on to get another job, than be too demotivated even to go after one.

SUCCESS THROUGH EFFECTIVE COMMUNICATION

Success is only achieved through people. This means that a manager or supervisor gets results not just from their own efforts–far greater results are achieved by duplication and from moulding people into a cohesive team.

Giving Instructions and Orders

Every supervisor and manager has to give other people instructions and orders from time to time. It is sometimes the case that these instructions are given at conferences or seminars, where senior managers have to lay out new strategy, methods of operation and in many cases changes of policy or even work practice. This is just as important as giving the instructions or orders themselves. The motivation required for the employees to implement the new strategy successfully was totally lacking and the reaction was negative, not positive. If only the managers had realized the importance of personal development training.

Instructions and orders do not necessarily always revolve around a change of work practice. But, in any circumstances, the manager should be using verbal communication to impart tasks or responsibility that lead towards the organization's collective goal.

Let's run through six ideas for giving instructions and orders that do get results, that do build the 'want' and that form a motivational style of management communication. The process is verbal and not written, although it can be followed up in some written form afterwards.

1. Make it clear what the order or instruction is.

   They often understand the situation so well themselves that they assume the other person knows what they are talking about.

2. How about getting people to repeat your instructions in their own words? Many people, on being given an instruction, will not admit that they do not fully understand all of what is being said or is expected of them, particularly if they feel their manager is impatient.

3. Encourage people to discuss and ask questions. Don't give the impression that you would be irritated or annoyed if a question were asked.

   By allowing people to ask questions, you increase their involvement and participation. This also reduces the risk of misunderstanding and develops opportunities for clarification. 'How do you feel about...?' 'What do you think?' 'Have you any ideas?'

4. Try asking rather than telling. The motivational manager knows he gets greater success through people by asking pleasantly rather than barking out an order.

   The 'Can you please dispatch that package today?' rather than 'I want that package dispatched today' or, even worse, 'Dispatch that package today'.

   'Will you please get that report completed by lunchtime?' is better than 'Get that report completed by lunchtime.'

   The way you ask people to do things makes such a difference, both to the relationship that develops between you and to the cooperation you will get. By asking, you will also avoid resentment.

5. Do tell the individual why. This can just be a brief explanation; when somebody understands why a certain instruction needs to be carried out, it not only makes their job more interesting, but will help them to understand your point of view more

effectively. A person who understands why they are carrying out a task is far less likely to make a mistake.

They will also become more committed and involved, and if the job becomes unnecessary, they will have enough sense not to continue. On the other hand, if they don't understand the reason for doing the job, they will blindly go on doing what they have been told to do.

6. Do follow up. Staying in touch is one of the most successful methods of preventing little problems from becoming much larger ones. It also has the added advantage that people will look forward to giving you information on their progress and it will encourage successful and positive results from them.

People hate imparting bad news to their manager, so if they know that they are going to be asked to discuss something, their commitment and determination to succeed will be so much stronger.

Careful handling is needed in certain situations.

Some people lack confidence, others are very sensitive or, at the other extreme, have an ego problem. Such people may have to be coached into believing that the idea or reason for the instruction was theirs.

The conversation can go something like 'How do you feel this should be handled?', and after their response, the reply can be 'I thought you were going to say that' or 'I thought that was what you were really thinking.'

DELEGATION

Success comes through people. The great leaders and

managers of the world surely have at least two things in common. First, they have a desire to employ people with greater skills or knowledge than they themselves possess, and secondly, they have an ability to develop people into leaders. In other words, they look for ways to duplicate themselves in other people.

Developing people is achieved by careful and planned delegation of responsibility and duty. No manager will ever achieve very much if they try to carry the whole burden of management on their shoulders.

There are four stages to successful delegation:

1. Assume that people who work for you have ability. Managers must make that assumption. They must have that confidence and belief in their subordinates. By showing that they have that confidence in their staff, most people will rise to the level of ability that their manager is assuming they have.

   We have said earlier: 'It is not ability but desire that creates success.' Abilities can be learned, and if a manager shows their own confidence in an individual's abilities, this will in turn increase the person's desire if the ability is at present limited.

2. When delegating a job, leave as little doubt as possible in the employee's mind as to what is expected. Tell the individual:

   (a) what should be done;

   (b) why it is needed;

   (c) when it should be completed.

3. *But do not tell them how.* This is the secret of successful delegation. When you tell somebody exactly how you want a task carried out, it removes any creativity. It becomes completely boring, there is no challenge and they do not have to develop in

any capacity whatsoever. But by not telling them how, it does create a challenge. It gets the brain working. It will no doubt create some stress or excitement, but it gives the individual a chance to think.

You might say 'My tasks are far too important to risk a mistake', in which case you can ask the person to work out the best way of tackling the task, but to check with you before actually proceeding. This, of course, does give you a safety net and perhaps fewer sleepless nights!

4. Finally, the motivational manager will, of course, always give credit and praise generously if a person does a good job.

   If, on the other hand, they do a lousy job (which is unlikely if you have followed the above stages), whatever you do, don't make a great deal of it. They will know they have done a lousy job. They will also have a lack of confidence, and if you are a motivational leader, they will almost certainly not make that mistake again. But the experience will have been an educational one through which they will be a greater asset and a better employee in the future.

SELECT READINGS

Alderfer, A., *Existence, Relatedness and Growth: Human Needs in Organizations*, New York, Free Press, 1972.

Anne Bruce, *How to Motivate Every Employee*, The McGraw-Hill Professional Education Series, Career Pr Inc, 2002.

Baumeister, R.F., Vohs, K.D. *Handbook of Self-regulation: Research, Theory, and Applications*, New York: Guilford Press. 2004.

Campbell, J.P. et.al., *Managerial Behaviour: Performance and Effectiveness*, McGraw-Hill, 1970.

Carver, C.S., Scheier, M.F., *On the Self-regulation of Behavior*, New York: Cambridge University Press. 2001.

Cofer, C.N. and Appley, M.H., *Motivation: Theory and Practice*, Wiley, 1964.

Emmons, R.A., *The Psychology of Ultimate Concerns: Motivation and Spirituality in Personality.* New York: Guilford Press. 2003.

Gellerman, S.W., *Motivation and Productivity*, American Management Association, 1963.

Hahn, C.P., *Dimensions of Job Satisfaction and Career Motivation*, Pittsburg, American Institute of Research, 1959.

Lawler, E.E., *Motivation in Work Organizations*, Brooks–Cole, 1973.

Locke, E. A. and Latham, G. P., *Goal Setting: A Motivational Technique that Works.* Englewood Cliffs, NJ: Prentice Hall. 1984.

Maslow, H. A., *Motivation and Personality.* New York: Harper and Rowe. 1987.

McClelland, D.C., *Human Motivation.* Cambridge: Cambridge University Press. 1987.

Miller, W. R. and Rollnick, S., (Eds.). *Motivational Interviewing* (2nd ed.) New York: Guilford Press. 2002.

Murphy, Jim, *Inner Excellence*, McGraw-Hill. 2009.

Patrick Forsyth, *How to Motivate People: Learn the Key Skills; Get the Best Results; Develop, Appraise, Empower (Creating Success)*, Kogan Page, 2010.

Paul, W.J. and Robertson, K.B., *Job Enrichment and Employee Motivation*, Gower Press, 1970.

Shia, Regina M., *Academic Intrinsic and Extrinsic Motivation and Metacognition. Assessing Academic Intrinsic Motivation: A Look at Student Goals and Personal Strategy*. Wheeling Jesuit University, 1998.

Stephen P. and Judge, Timothy A., *Essentials of Organizational Behavior* (9 ed.), Upper Saddle River, NJ: Prentice Hall. 2007.

Steve Chandler and Scott Richardson, *100 Ways to Motivate Others: How Great Leaders Can Produce Insane Results Without Driving People Crazy*, Career Press, 2008.

Weightman, J., *The Employee Motivation Audit*, Cambridge Strategy Publications. 2008.

Winter, D.G., "Power Motivation Revisited". In C. P. Smith (ed.), *Motivation and Personality: Handbook of Thematic Content Analysis*, New York: Cambridge University. 1992.

Wong, R., *Motivation: A Biobehavioural Approach*, Cambridge: Cambridge University Press. 2000.

Other Books on
MANAGEMENT

Unit No. 220, Second Floor, 4735/22,
Prakash Deep Building,Ansari Road, Daryaganj,
New Delhi- 110002, Ph.: 32903912, 23280047, 09811838000
• E-mail : lotus_press@sify.com. www.lotuspress.co.in